To Renee
with best wi...
Fred...

My Songs of
Now and Then

My Songs of
Now and Then

A Memoir

Rachel Josefowitz Siegel

iUniverse, Inc.
Bloomington

My Songs of Now and Then
A Memoir

iUniverse books may be ordered through booksellers or by contacting:

iUniverse
1663 Liberty Drive
Bloomington, IN 47403
www.iuniverse.com
1-800-Authors (1-800-288-4677)

ISBN: 978-1-4759-3383-3 (sc)
ISBN: 978-1-4759-3382-6 (hc)
ISBN: 978-1-4759-3381-9 (ebk)

Library of Congress Control Number: 2012911313

Printed in the United States of America

iUniverse rev. date: 08/29/2012

Contents

SNAPSHOTS OF LOVED ONES: OUR FAMILY

MORE LOVED ONES: PARENTS AND SIBLINGS

FRIENDS

HEIRLOOMS AND RECIPES

SEASONS

WHIMSICAL NOTES

OLDER AND WISER

LIFE JOURNEYS AND PERSONAL DEVELOPMENT

This book is dedicated
to the memory of
Benjamin Morton Siegel, 1916-1990,
my beloved husband and life partner.

Family Tree

Josefowitz and Siegel Ancestors

George S Gregory
(Grisha) Josefowitz *1894-1984*
Lydia Schlossberg

Peter Gregory
Alex Gregory *b1925*
Angre Gregory *b1934*
Chiquita *first wife* Cindy Klein *second wife*

Mendel Chaim Joseph *b1871*
Lena

Fruma Josefowitz *d1975*
Petia (Peter) Fliegers

Serge (Isac. J.) Fliegers *b1923-1998*

Charles (Chazkel) Josefowitz *1891-1944*
Fania Choronshitski *1905-1996*

Mira Josefowitz *b1928*
Eryk Spektor *1921-1998*

Shneir Zalman Josefowitz *1861-1939*
Chaya Podkovik *1857-1942*

Fenny Josefowitz *b1931*
Benjamin Oren *b1930*

Rachel (Rochel Gitel) Josefowitz *b1924*

Pincus Zelig (Zachar) Josefowitz *1889-1949*
Frieda Shur *1890-1984*

Benjamin Morton Siegel *b1916-1990*

Samuel (Mulik) Josefowitz *b1922*
Natasha Chapro *b1925 divorced*

David (Dodik) Josefowitz *b1919*
Tanya Kagan *b1925*

Chatzkel Yankel Josefowitz *b1834*
Khaya Reyza *b1836*

Rokhlya Josefowitz *1857*

Frada Josefowitz *1886-1960*
Beprosvani

Rose Josefowitz *b1917*
Yasha Choron (Choronjitski) *divorced*

Lazar Best

Velvel (William) Joseph *1885-1930*
Pearl Green *1886-1974*

Ruth Joseph *b1920*
Benson Moskowitz *1926-1984*

Sara B Joseph *1926-2002*
Otto Lefkowitz, *dtr*

David Joseph *1924*
Joan Altdstetter *1930*

Leonard Joseph *b1921 d.1988*
Pamela Reece *b1935*

Beylya Josefowitz *1855*

Frieda I Joseph *1919*
Abraham Kaplan *1912-2001*

Charles J Joseph *1916-1997*
Naomi Veve *1933*

Isadore Joseph *1912-1965*

Wulf Josefowitz

Sonia (Sora) Josefowitz *d1942*
Tamarkin

Chaim Tamarkin
Ludmila Kutergina

Mania Tamarkin *d2005*
Fred Bock-Bordy

Tamara Tamarkin *1911-1979*
Herman (Chuck) Rosen

Dov Beryl (Bera) Josefowitz
Gita Zalk *d1888*
Etel Afroim *second wife*

Pauline (Pesha) Josephs *1888-1975*
Aaron (Yewofski) Siegel *1870-1951*
Etta (Elkah) Bloom *1871-1913*
First Marriage of Aaron Siege

Gita Siegel *1920-2012*
Abraham Braude *1917-1984*

Kathryn Jane Braude *b1940*
d 1995 William Rothbart *b1950 divorced*
Lucien Wulsin *second marriage*

Claire Susan Frances Braude *1945-2002*

Sarah Josephs
Sachna Josephs *1861-1930*
Louis Y Josephs *1862-1928*
Benjamin Josephs *1865-1902*
Hyman Josephs *1869-1948*

Benjamin Morton Siegel *1916-1990*
Rachel (Rochel Gitel) Josefowitz *b1924*

Benjamin Siegel *1906-1913*

Sylvia (Sophia) Siegel *1889-1913*

Philip Siegel *1909-1913*

Nathan Siegel *b1907-1991*
Elsie Orenstein *1903-1995*

Joan Siegel *b1933*
Arthur Rubenstein *divorced*
Jack Abrahamson *second husband*

Edward Ellis Siegel *1929-2006*
Joan Ribenzer *divorced*
Jean Eddy *divorced*
Audra Keller

Rachel and Benjamin Siegel's Descendants

Etta (Elkah) Bloom
1871-1913
First Marriage

Aaron (Yewofski) Siegel
1870-1951

Pauline (Pesha) Josephs
(second wife) 1888-1975

- **Nathan Siegel** *1901-1991*
  Elsie Orenstein *1903-1995*
  - **Joan Siegel** *b1933*
    Arthur Rubenstein *divorced*
    Jack Abrahamson *second husband*
    - Lynn Audrey *b1967*
      Amit Sela *div.*
      James General Nicholson
      - Amalia Nicholson *b1987*
      - Zev Avrahan Nicholson *b1989*
    - Sally Annette Rubenstein *b1958*
      Gregory Vinje *divorced*
      Daniel Drescher *second husband*
      - Justin Paul Vinje *b1981*
      - Shane Allen Vinje *b1985*
      - Jacob Samuel Vinje *b1988*
    - John Aaron Rubenstein *b1958*
    - Michael Oren Rubenstein *b1961*
      Gail Leervig
  - **Edward Ellis Siegel** *1929-2006*
    Joan Ribenzer *divorced*
    Jean Eddy *divorced*
    Audra Keller
    - Timothy Siegel *b1968*
      Kimberly Bayer
    - Paul Siegel *b1966*
      Cella Long
    - David Siegel *b1964*

- **Gita Siegel** *1920-2012*
  Abraham Braude *1917-1984*
  - **Kathryn Jane Braude** *b1949*
    William Rothbart *b1950 divorced*
    Lucien Wulsin *second marriage*
    - Lisa Rose Rothbart *b1982*
    - Benjamin Braude Rothbart *b1986* Lyndee Radenbaugh *b1982*
  - **Claire Susan Frances Braude** *1945-2002*

- **Benjamin Morton Siegel** *b1976-1990*
  Rachel (Rochel Gitel) Josefowitz *b1924*

Pincus Zelig (Zachar) Josefowitz *1889-1949*
Frieda Shur *1890-1984*

- **Fenny Josefowitz** *b1931*
  Benjamin Oren *b1930*
  - **Ariel Oren** *b1969*
    Eti
    - Aviv
    - Mayan
  - **Zecharia (Kaya) Emmanuel Oren** *b1955*
    Susan Lynne Steinberg *b1959*
    - Lena Frieda Oren *b1994*
    - Aleksander Geffen Oren *b1992*
  - **Galila Oren** *b1957*
    Doriel Tabatchnikov *b1951*
    - Noriel Tabatchnikov
    - Noga Tabatchnikov *b1993*
    - Noam Tabatchnikov *b1990*

- **Rachel (Rochel Gitel) Josefowitz** *b1924*
  Benjamin Morton Siegel *1916-1990*
  - **Ruth Vivian Siegel** *b1950*
    - Thomas Aaron Siegel *b1978*
      Sarah Brown *b1982*
      - Maxwell Harper Siegel *b2004*
      - Rylan Sidney Siegel *b2005*
    - Brenda Lynn Siegel *b1976*
      - Ajna Johnathon Misch Siegel *b2002*
    - Johnathon Siegel *1971-1996*
      Heather Maples
      - Kaya Benjamin Siegel *b1992*
  - **Hyam Barry Siegel** *b1948*
    Judy Kinoy *divorced*
  - **Charles Elias Siegel** *b1946*
    Cheryl Pierson *b1945*
    - Anna Rebecca Siegel *b1981*
    - Sarah Helen Pnina Siegel *b1978*
      Alan Tse *b1978*

- **Samuel (Mulik) Josefowitz** *b1922*
  Natasha Chapro *b1925 divorced*
  - **Paul Zachary Josefowitz** *b1952*
    Ellen Melas Kyriazi
    - Nicholas Josefowitz
      Tali Rapaport
    - Laura Hava Josefowitz Shell *b1980*
  - **Nina Josefowitz** *b1950*
    Bryan Shell *divorced*
    David Douglas Myran *b1549 second husband*
    - Daniel Thomas Josefowitz Myran *b1988*
    - Aaron Frazer Josefowitz Myran *b1987*
  - **Cathryn Dianne Josefowitz** *b1956*
    Beppe (Joseppe) Sebaste *divorced*
    - Pierre Sebaste *b1991*
    - Marco Benatoff

- **David (Dodik) Josefowitz** *b1919*
  Tanya Kagan *b1925*
  - **Victoria Anne Josefowitz** *b1952*
    Coby (Jacob) Benatoff
    - Alex Benatoff
      Laura
      - Lisa Benatoff
      - Eva Benatoff
      - Sasha Benatoff
    - Andrea Benatoff
      Cecilia
      - Stella Benatoff
      - Sarah Tanya Benatoff

- **Rose Josefowitz** *b1917*
  Yasha Choron (Choronjitski) *divorced*
  - **Polly Josefowitz** *b1950*
    Christoph Hering *b1947*
    - Melanie Pearl Hering *b1990*
    - Michael (Misha) Jonah Hering *b1986*

Frieda Shur/Lurie(a) Family

Frieda Shur
1890-1984
Pincus Zelig
(Zachar) Josefowitz
1889-1949

Fenny Josefowitz b1931
Benjamin Oren b1930

Rachel (Rochel Gitel) Josefowitz b1924
Benjamin Morton Siegel
1916-1990

Samuel (Mulik) Josefowitz b1922
Natasha Chapro b1925 divorced

David (Dodik) Josefowitz b1919
Tanya Kagan b1925

Rose Josefowitz b1917
Yasha Choron (Choronjitski) divorced

Hinde Shur
Volosov

Rochel (Ray) Volosof 1926-1997
Nachman Kronenberg 1920-2006

Philip Volosov d2006
Beverly div.
Heidy (second wife)

Gitel (Jean) Shur Volosov b1921
Eli Einbinder

Nathan Eleazar
Shur 1911-?
Miriam b1906

Ray (Rachel) Shur 1933
Robert Widder 1926-2008

Vivian Shur
? First husband
Gerald Wolff sec. husband

Chaim Shur
Chaya Epstein
Rabbi Nathan
Nata Lurie(a)
b1820

Rabbi Eliahu
Jacob Dov Shur
1848-1936
Rochel Gitel Lurie
1850-1923

Rabbi Moshe
Mishel Lurie
b1790

Saul Luria b1760

Rabbi Solomon
Luria 1510-1573

RASHI 1040-1105

Hyman Shur
Minnie Green

Herbert Frootko 1919-1995
Joy Kaplan d2003

Ann Frootko 1917-1969
George Behrmann 1909-1962

Frieda Frotko 1913-1983
Joe Kapelus

Sarah Eisman Shur
1911-1982
Israel Frootko d1953

Jan (Isaac) Frootko 1907-2000
Maxine (div.)

Ronnie (Rose) Shur 1920-2008
Abraham Cohen 1910-1998

Ethel Shur 1918-2012
Saul Harold Sinkoff 1918-2001

Saul Shur 1915-1983
Sarah Eva Hamer (Hamburger) 1917-1982

Mishel Meyer Shur
1875-1943
Dora (Dveirel)Rebecca
Golombok 1882-1957

Sadie Shur 1913-2006
Isadore Goren 1909-1981

Nathan Eleazar Shur b1911
Sarah Eisman 1911-1992

Herzl Shur 1905-1992
Rose Lipsitz 1911-2006

Acknowledgments

My songs of now and then were written on Tuesday mornings in Zee's Writing Circle. There, surrounded by sister writers, I filled four large notebooks of musings and memories over a period of seven years. Urged on by Zee's weekly "sparks," we wrote, we listened, and we learned from each other. My heartfelt thanks to Irene Zahava, whose weekly encouragement, enthusiasm, and creative energy inspired the writing of nearly all the vignettes and haikus in this collection.

Chelly Siegel, Nina Miller, and Mira Spektor confirmed my hesitant beginnings by reading early drafts of the manuscript. Members of the John Munchauer Writers Group at Kendal supported me with their interest and gentle feedback as I began to assemble the essays into a book. This was a task more difficult and complex than the writing of it.

I am immensely grateful to my editorial consultants. Emily Rhoads Johnson helped me in the first selection and organization of pieces out of the handwritten notebooks. Linda Myers reviewed and edited the next draft with critical expertise, suggesting major additions and minor deletions. Irene Zahava's reading added the finishing refinements.

Sarah Siegel designed the book cover.

Last but not least, I am grateful to my extended family, my dear *mishpochah*, whose impact on my life permeates these pages. To my children, grandchildren, and great-grandchildren, whose existence fills me with deepest joy and whose delightful visits and occasional concerns have given me food for thought while occasionally interrupting my writing and creativity.

To Benjamin Siegel, my beloved husband of forty-six years, more thanks than I can put into words for enriching my life with his presence and exposing me to the habit of critical thinking, intellectual pursuits, and the joys of sailing.

Rachel Josefowitz Siegel, February 22, 2012

ABOUT THIS BOOK

How I Started to Write

In 1979, when I was fifty-five, I sat by the pool in Hawaii on a sunny day in January and made a wish list. It started with this: *I want to write. I want to write and collect articles for a book.*

It was a written commitment in a brand-new notebook that held nothing else in it. That year I attended a writing workshop followed by a summer group therapy workshop in which I was invited to state my goal. Easy: "I want to write. To overcome some of the inhibitions and procrastinating patterns that keep me from doing so."

That was the beginning. It all started with a wish. For many years I wrote professional articles and collaborated with other therapists at the Feminist Therapy Institute. We did books together, edited one another's work, mentored each other, and created a network of feminist writers. We were not afraid of the F word; we flaunted it rather brazenly. As time went on, my voice got softer, less angry perhaps, more personal.

After my retirement it was time for a new wish, a new goal. I wanted to switch from professional writing to personal writing. My first year of Tuesday morning sessions in Zee's Writing Circle resulted in a small collection of essays assembled for my family. Now, in the year 2012, I am in my fifth notebook. The first two were loose-leaf. Now they are hardbound, a conscious switch from "just writing" to "writing and keeping." No more pages torn out in displeasure.

The essays in this book are bits of my personal truth. No book can ever pretend to be the whole truth, and this one was never so intended. Roald Hoffman, poet and Nobel Prize–winning Cornell chemist, paraphrases an old *midrash*: "The jar of truth was shattered in heaven long ago; it is our task to gather the shards, the fragments, the pieces of truth."

Here they are, fragments of my truth, to share with loved ones, perhaps to make you laugh, or cry. Here they are, to let you glimpse into my life, my thoughts and feelings, my memories, my dreams. Here they are.

What I Write About

I write about my recollections—my wandering thoughts, feelings, and the seemingly useless ways I sometimes spend my time and energy. I ponder and write about what I do with my time, how much I do for others and with others, and how much I do for myself.

I write about the *kein an horah* syndrome: the need to find the flaw when all is well, when things are good, when happiness is palpable. *Kein an horah*, no evil eye, don't let the neighbors know your happiness, your joy, and your abundance. Don't make them envious; don't tempt the angel of death.

I sing and rejoice in the glory of my garden, the orange poppy, the white peony, the rose bush starting to bloom, the tall ferns under the plum tree, and the solitary pleasure when beauty feeds my soul. I take pen to paper, shouting with joy at the Japanese maple who has recovered her former glory because I gave her food last year.

In this book I write about the gardens of my life, the loves and friendships, the blooming and fading of deep relationships. I write about memories and blessings, pains and losses. I write about the feel and colors of each season, the long winters and sudden springs, the lazy summers and glorious autumns. I write about the journeys of my life, journeys in space and in personal development, growing up and growing old and older yet.

I write about life—no more, no less. Life as I have lived it with its peculiarities, mistakes, accomplishments, rewards and accidents, changes and constancy.

Yes, life is what I write about—no more, no less.

My Song

I once wrote a song of the earth. I wrote it during a long winter of loss and depression, after my husband's first heart attack. The earth sang to me with hope and consolation. Today, I write a song of myself.

These vignettes of my life, written in haste every Tuesday morning at Zee's Writing Circle, these songs of myself, isolated in time and place, are pulled together by the recurrent themes of my long life.

Is it a song of myself or to myself? At times it feels self-indulgent, this persistent urge, so strong, to leave a testament of who I am and who I have been. What makes me think that it might have meaning to my sons, my daughter? Could I, in creating this mythology of self and family, be leaving a gift to my grandchildren and their descendants, the gift of their own history perhaps? Do they want to know as much as I want to tell? Does my own need to recapture and tell the facts and memories of my life, filtered as they are through my own perceptions, have meaning for someone else? I like to think it does. But even if it does not, this song of self is important to me, if only for myself alone.

It is a song of now and then, of how it all got started, of belonging and not belonging. I write of times when I can't find my laughter in searching the inner garden of my soul. There are nights, alone in bed and half asleep, when I feel your presence, Ben, as if you were still next to me. I replay the myth of you and I, sometimes with joy, sometimes with sorrow, always with longing; holding on to the feel of your body against mine, the odor of your hair, the touch of your hands, and the sweetness of your tongue. This is my private song, a precious memory, unlisted in the inventory of my life's blessings. It is not a family secret, yet deeply private. Yes, Grandma still has sexual memories and fantasies worth singing about. So let me break the fences of conventionality and enrich the song of my life by humming even a private melody.

The fences are still there, getting in the way of knowing and telling and singing out loud. Conventionality and fear of envy keep the joys subdued. The fear of the evil eye, *kein an hora*, exerts a powerful inhibition to the singing of my blessings, my good fortune, my accomplishments. Who can I trust to be glad with me and not judgmental, not jealous or disparaging?

"Who does she think she is? Bragging like that, she's so full of herself, self-centered. It's always about her." "Women and children should be seen and not heard." Or: "Be careful, the Angel of Death might hear you. The neighbors might take revenge." *"Mon tor nit oiskratzen di oigen,"* my mother would say. "One should not scratch out their eyes (with envy)."

Hide your wealth, don't brag, never count your children out loud. The fence gets in the way, made up of loud phrases all around me, a cacophony of sexist messages and Jewish paranoia that is rooted in not-so-ancient fears of pogroms and persecutions.

But now is now, and the song of myself wants to be sung. If I could not sing or write, I would never again find my laughter; I would be silenced into waiting only for the end.

GLIMPSES OF
CHILDHOOD MEMORIES

Preussen Allee 15, Berlin

My Homes

1924, Berlin
Hot summer day
I was born

Preussen Allee 15
Age one to six
Wide garden steps

1930, Château du Signal
Lausanne
Learning French

Chemin du Levant
Up the big tree
Sam climbed higher

1935, Zürich, Volta Strasse
Chinese sitting room
Schwyzerdütsch

Lausanne again
Pensionat La Ramée
Girls everywhere

1938
Avenue don't remember
Change and fear

1939 Hotel in New York
Seasick all the way
Saddle shoes

Montreal
Alice in Wonderland
Red plaid skirt

Cambridge, Mrs. Henri's Dorm
Scared girl acting grown-up
Alone

1940, Simmons North Hall
High heel alligator shoes
Dating

Evans Hall, fifth floor
Necking until curfew
In love

1944, Cambridge, Riverside Drive
Sex before breakfast, after lunch
Newly wed

Linneaen Street
Third-floor walk-up
Heavy groceries

1945, Shady Hill Square
First child miracle
New mother

Eastern Parkway
Tante Hinde, Brooklyn Park
Strange world

285 Central Park West
My parents' home
Not mine

Summer in Mahopac
Hot and heavy
Pregnant again

1948, Old Cambridge House
Two sons now
Papa died

1949, Ithaca, Fall Creek Drive
Green hat, white gloves
Faculty wife

Hanshaw Road
Blue chintz curtains
Baby Ruth

1956 Avenue Charles Floquet
Americans in Paris
Morning baguette

203 Forest Drive
Teenagers, picnics
Shouts and whispers

Taughannock Boulevard rental
Peaches and sunshine
Joy

1960, Kikar Wingate, Jerusalem
Almond blossoms in January
Jewish among Jews

1975, Taughannock Boulevard
Built dream house
Midlife honeymoon

Spruce Lane, Ithaca

1992, Spruce Lane
My bed, my garden, my desk
Myself alone

2007, Savage Farm Drive
Life with people again
Community

2011, Kendal apartment
Joys, aches, blessings
Old, still kicking

Running Away

Once I ran away from home and into the woods. It was the day my sister was born, and my five-year-old self was full of unknown feelings, feelings so powerful, so scary, and so misunderstood. By me? By others? By all? No one had told me why Mutti was away in a hospital. My brothers teased me for not knowing that a new baby was on the way.

The woman who had come to do the laundry was the only one who took me in her arms, who made me feel a bit more comfortable. When she left at the end of the day, I couldn't bear being without her. I followed her, near enough to see where she was going, far enough so she would not detect me and take me home. But I lost her among the many paths through the woods. The trees were dark and tall. I smelled the leaves, the strong earth smell.

I was tired and scared but still willful. I was more scared of being found and punished than of being lost. When they came and called my name, I hid and did not answer. It was David, no longer teasing me, who gently coaxed me out of hiding and took me back home.

My First Train Ride

I was six years old when my family traveled from Berlin to Vienna to visit my grandparents and to show them my new baby sister, Fenny. It was an overnight journey by train. Mutti and I slept in a sleeping compartment, the baby next to me on the same berth, in a well-padded sleeping basket. I do not remember how Papa, Rose, David, and Sam were distributed, but I vaguely recall that we had adjoining compartments. I was fascinated by the tiny sink and water closet, scared of the noisy flush of the toilet. Could I get sucked right out of the train and onto the tracks?

My only recollection of the actual Vienna visit was being taken to the "Prater," the giant amusement park with the equally giant and most frightening Ferris wheel. My brothers were eager and excited to go on that ride and teased me when I said I was too scared to join them. I was much relieved when my reluctance was accepted and they gave up trying to persuade me. Their teasing did not stop.

Lausanne

I think of Lausanne as my hometown. Though we moved frequently, from town to town and from country to country, my fondest memories are of Lausanne. The hills, the lake, the big house called Château du Signal, and later, the first-floor apartment and garden at 7 Chemin du Levant.

The day we moved into Château du Signal in 1930, I remember my mother standing at the kitchen table in this cavernous room, slicing big chunks of peasant bread. She held the fragrant round loaf against her chest, large knife in hand, and I was sure she would cut herself. Of course she didn't. She offered hefty slices of bread and butter with cheese and mustard to the burly moving men during their morning break. They spoke French; she did not and neither did I.

I was six years old and full of wonder and excitement. So many new impressions. Who ever heard of cheese and mustard on the same piece of bread? I sensed my mother's power, her competence, taking charge in this unfamiliar land and language, and directing the men to place our belongings where she wanted them to be.

A few years later we moved to Chemin du Levant. It was a large apartment, large enough to accommodate our parents, five children, a nanny, and a cook. There was a smaller apartment over the garage, occupied by the chauffeur.

On school days, I eagerly ran downhill to L'École Supérieure de Jeunes Filles.

On the way I passed a small park where I often stopped to play. The park was long and narrow and held a double row of chestnut trees. It was dark under the majestic trees, dark and mysterious, lighter toward the middle of this alley where the branches did not quite meet. In spring, the large clusters of white flowers tinged with pink seemed almost supernatural. Later, as seasons passed, chestnuts appeared in their prickly outer shells and dropped to the ground where I could pick them up. The challenge was not so much finding them as opening these outer shells. That was a messy, difficult operation and darkened my hands every time. Were we even allowed to pick them? I remember only a sense of furtiveness and an almost irresistible attraction.

Quite often I arrived at school just as the opening bell began to ring and was lucky enough to enter my classroom before the sound of the bell ended. Safe from a tardy mark.

I passed the park every day on my way to school. On the way back up the hill, I rode the tram. Home for lunch, the big meal of the day, and down the hill again.

When school was out in the afternoon, I nearly always stopped at the pâtisserie for a delicious treat. Sometimes I just stood in front of the store trying to decide if I was hungry enough to indulge. When my allowance ran short I had to make a choice between a sweet treat followed by a long walk up the hill or no treat and the ease of riding the tram.

These were weighty daily decisions. First, did I have enough money left for a pastry, and if so, which of the delectable items should I choose, with their tempting aromas of almond, chocolate, and vanilla wafting out to the street? And then, walk or tram. I would walk if I had a friend or classmate to walk with me and make the hike less dull and tiresome. I chose the tram depending on the weather and how tired I felt. If I dawdled too long in front of the pâtisserie, I might find the later tram ride crowded and have to stand, hanging on to one of the straps. For some reason, it is the memory of these decisions that stays with me: decisions, decisions, indulgence or deprivation, exercise or comfort. It's a dilemma I have not yet outgrown.

Pully Plage

I must have been eleven years old when I took the little winding path downhill toward Lac Léman. It was a hot day in August, and I had permission to go swimming alone at the supervised public beach in Pully. In those days we were not chauffeured all over town, and I was accustomed to finding my way around, walking up and down the hills of Lausanne. But I was not really familiar with the *sentier* that started just below my home. Would it really lead me to my destination? But hey, I was a Girl Scout, *une éclaireuse*, I would surely figure it out when I got there. And I did.

Oh, how grown-up I felt when I paid the entrance fee and found a spot among the older teenagers. Was that the day I tasted my first Coke? I can still feel the cold bottle in my hand and taste the sweet bubbly stuff—another sign of growing up. Alone among many, I had no word for the slight unease, the bravado, the pretense of wanting to look older than my years, the excitement of it all.

The swimming area was crowded; so many bodies confined to a limited roped-off space. I felt frustration and safety both. As my suntanned body moved smoothly through the coolness of this bit of lake, I relished the harmony of self and nature. Then, on dry land again, soaking up the afternoon sun, I contemplated the long trek back up the hill, feeling elated at my lone adventure.

Anti-Semitism in a New School

When we moved to Zürich from Lausanne, I encountered my first male teacher in sixth grade. I was coping with a new school, in a new language. Not only did I have to switch from French to German, but the informal speech in the schoolyard was Schwyzerdütsch, the local version of an old German dialect, which I tried to quickly absorb.

One day, during recess, some girls wanting perhaps to get to know this new kid, questioned me about really being able to speak French. They wanted to know if I could swear in French, and to prove it, would I do it right now? The words that came out of my mouth were "*sale crétin*" literally translated as "dirty retard" or a person of low IQ. The shocked response was palpable. The girls turned away from me and ran to tell the teacher. What they had misheard was "*sale Chrétien*," translated "dirty Christian." No wonder they were upset!

In class, the teacher marched up to me, confronted me, and refused to accept my explanation. I did not know the German word for *crétin*, but he did not want to believe me. He slapped my face and called me "*sale Juive*" translated as "dirty Jewess."

My life in that classroom was never the same after that. I made no friends. At home, my parents, less familiar with French and unfamiliar with the word *crétin*, could not understand why that had to be the one dangerous word I had chosen to use. Why not some other swear word? Well, truth to tell, I didn't know many other words to swear with in any language other than Yiddish, perhaps, or Russian, which I could have heard my parents use, but never knew the meaning of.

1937 Hirschengraben Secundar Schule

I flunked the oral exam that separates college-bound kids from the others at the end of sixth grade. I had nearly peed in my pants, waiting for my turn in the corridor before appearing before this panel of stuffy Schwyzerdütsch male examiners. Having changed schools and languages the year before, I was as insecure as I have ever been in my now eighty-seven years of life, and spent the next two years being miserable. Often bored to death, yet only second in my class, because Heidi, the teacher's daughter, always came in first.

The adolescent boys did not overtly mingle with the girls; some of them were repeating seventh grade. I remember one gangly youth who had outgrown his pants; he was good looking, but clearly not at ease in a school setting. I made friends with Evie Heim, a Jewish girl who lived near us, and Ilse Braun. Lilly was another

Jewish girl whom we befriended after she suddenly lost her mother (to suicide, it was hinted). She was the daughter of a hairdresser, a single mom, and lived in a tiny apartment in the poorer section of town, a world I had never even glimpsed before. She was pretty, with short black hair and straight bangs. She appeared more mature, more sexy, and far more unhappy than any girl I had ever come to know before. I wonder what became of her.

It was an awkward age and an uneasy time, with Hitler in power next door in Germany. Our family were legal residents of Switzerland, a visiting status that could be revoked. War was in the air, we had blackout drills. And I, newly menstruating, feeling all the normal confusion and awkwardness of my changing body, was trying to adjust and find a place of belonging, a semblance of "normal" life.

I had to deal with being Jewish when Jewish was becoming more and more unsafe in my world. How could I blend in, in my Swiss Girl Scout troop? I remember the deep longing to be like them, to enjoy the candle lighting of the Christmas tree in the forest without feeling Jewish guilt and reservations. And I remember the moment of strangeness and deep shame when I realized that the song I had joined in singing in the girls' locker room was the German song of Nazi allegiance, the "*Horst Wessel Lied*."

Looking back, I know that my frequent migraines were evidence of a deeper malaise, a subtle depression and a stubborn will to succeed in juggling my conflicting feelings and insecurities. During our school outings and excursions into the Swiss mountains, I couldn't help pretending that the camaraderie of my schoolmates and the glorious beauty all around us was mine as much as theirs. Yet there would always be, beneath the surface, the knowledge that this was but an illusion, and my otherness would surface.

My First Concert

I remember my first concert. I was thirteen years old, and it was a very special gala event. Hephzibah and Yehudi Menuhin, sister and brother, were performing in the Zürich Concert Hall. My parents were excited about this prodigy, a talented Jewish violinist accompanied by his equally talented sister. We would all attend.

In those days it was customary to dress up for such occasions. The seamstress came to the house; clothes were fitted and ordered. The day arrived. I wore my very first evening gown, pale green silk with puffed sleeves, and shiny new patent leather shoes. I do not remember what they played, but it was most beautiful. I was entranced by the music and immersed in my own fantasy of being my own brother's accompanist. Since Hephzibah was only a few years older than I, it seemed possible. I thought that I could play as well in another three or four years, having already had several years of piano studies. I imagined us onstage. I adored my older brother David, whose violin playing was superb.

This fantasy nourished my imagination for several days or weeks, but my piano playing did not improve. As a matter of fact, my sister Rose played much better than I. Reality set in and I soon neglected the extra hours of practice, but continued to cherish the fantasy. In my daydreams, David in tuxedo and I in a ball gown, made glorious music on the world's stages. In my secret longings, I played as well as Hephzibah, and I skated as well as Sonja Henie.

Rachel   Rose, David, Fenny, Rachel

Arosa

It was a very special, sunny winter day in Arosa when
I followed my older brothers up the ski trail, proud,
oh so proud to be allowed on this advanced excursion.
No more kiddie slope for me. I wore seal skins on the
bottom of my skis to keep me from slipping downhill as
I trekked up the mountain.

We stopped for a rest far above the timberline. I
took off my heavy outer sweater and wrapped it around
my waist. We shared our chocolate bar and prepared for

the quick run down the slope, nearly blinded by virgin snow.

The feeling of elation and control is with me still. The memory is in my bones and in my heart. I feel the wind on my face and relive the brilliant reflection of sun on fresh snow. My knees and legs remember the tension of dipping to the right, then to the left, guiding the skis with the weight of my body. The alp was mine, the wind my very own, mine and my brothers' as they whizzed by, shouting for joy. I was queen of the mountain.

As I write this, I am eighty-six years old. It is again a sunny winter day. I sit by my window, looking out at the snowy Kendal landscape and worry about the short walk to the main building for my Sunday brunch. Will I be able to keep my balance against the puffs of wind? Should I use my cane or my walker?

Back then, I loved being active and outdoors, hiking steep mountain paths, biking up and down the streets of Zürich, running on the beach, swimming into the ocean waves. Now I shiver at the very thought of doing these things. I huff and puff on the shortest incline. I have not been on a bike in decades and gave up skiing long ago. Swimming, however, still gives me pleasure. In our calm indoor pool I can still feel the joy, the power, and the flexibility of my body.

SNAPSHOTS OF LOVED ONES:
OUR FAMILY

Naches and tsorres
Joys and worries
Life with people

Zachar & Frieda Josefowitz, Rachel, Ben,
Pauline & Aaron Siegel, Our Wedding, 6/15/1944

Ruth   Charles, Barry

Chelly, Charles   Ruth
Charles' Wedding 8/8/1975

Johnathon, Hyam Barry

Ben, Rachel,
6/15/1969,
photo Hyam Siegel

Hyam Barry, Ruth,
Charles, Rachel, 2002

Chelly,
Sarah, Anna,
Charles

Ben on *Seagull*

Ben at desk

Ben in Hawaii

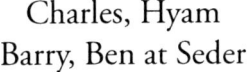

Charles, Hyam
Barry, Ben at Seder

Our Wedding

It was the beginning of summer. June, early June, a time for endings and beginnings, a time for graduations and weddings. My parents did not attend my Simmons graduation in Boston, being too busy planning my New York wedding three days later, June 15, 1944, to be precise.

My husband, Benjamin Morton Siegel, with a recent PhD from MIT, had been my brother David's fraternity brother. Ben was born and grew up in Superior, Wisconsin. His mother, Pauline, born Pauline

Josefowitz in Lithuania, was distantly related to my father. I was the first in my family to get married, and although it was wartime, I had a lavish wedding at the Park Lane Hotel in New York.

I remember so little of the preparations. Unlike many girls and young women, I had not fantasized about my wedding day, never played bride, and attended only one wedding before my own. I had hardly been involved in the elaborate plans made for me—or was it for them—by my parents and older sister Rose, with very little input from me. I would have just as soon eloped. I was so young, so much in love, the ceremony and celebration felt utterly unimportant.

I do remember asking Aunt Minnie to help me choose my lovely white gown at Jordan Marsh in Boston. And I remember Ben and I planning our honeymoon with playful anticipation, and the fun of keeping it a secret. The wedding would be on a Thursday, and we had the whole weekend for a honeymoon in the Berkshires. It was wartime, no time for a lengthy wedding trip.

What I do remember most vividly, with body, mind, and soul, is being in love with Ben, the physical urgency of our mutual touching, and the sense of being alone together on our own planet, in our own world of dreams and hopes. Walking the streets of Boston, hand in hand, sneaking a hug or a kiss, but never in public. I remember the cab ride to City Hall in New York the day before the wedding, squeezing Ben's hand hard enough to hurt him.

The ceremony itself is almost a blur, but I remember suppressing a giggle when circling the groom seven times in Jewish tradition. And then the night at the Hotel St. Moritz, making love, it seemed, all night long, watching the dawn come up over Central Park, and my amusement when Ben brushed his hair before getting back in bed. That night marked the beginning of intimacies collected over the years of living together; memories, gestures held consciously and unconsciously, absorbed and stored in the new sense of coupledness.

The *Seagull*

Thirty years later, the boat was always there on hot summer days when my body slid into the cool, inviting lake. The *Seagull* was moored just far enough offshore as a destination for a good swim. On the days when I swam along the shore to our neighbor's dock, she was there, keeping me company, a beacon, a visual cue keeping me on course.

The *Seagull* was also lovingly known as *Ben's Folly*. It was his dream boat. The year before his first heart attack, we had borrowed the Wilsons' sailboat while they were on sabbatical and started sailing out of the small East Shore Marina, just the two of us. Ben taught me to climb surefooted all over the deck and hull, adjusting the sails, becoming more confident of my own agility, overcoming my fears and hesitations. We loved sharing the feel of wind on water, and the intimacy of sun-drenched hours together.

When we returned from our own sabbatical in 1962, after Ben's heart attack, I suggested one dark spring day that we take a look at the boatyard. I wanted desperately to give Ben a ray of hope, to break through his lethargic, depressed mood. It worked. He fell in love with a nineteen-foot sailboat. We moored it at the inlet that first year, near what used to be Old Port Harbor. Years later we built our own summer house on the West Shore. We sailed from there, in a world of ever-changing hues of blue and white in sky and water.

I never did absorb the sailing words, and I still confuse *fore* and *aft*. For some unknown reason my linguistic facility with other languages did not apply. I do know terms like *beam* and *spinnaker*. I do know what to do when the captain shouts "Coming about!" But that's as far as it goes. Like any good crew, I did learn to man (or woman) the rudder and to follow orders. But I stubbornly resisted any attempt to have me take over. I needed to let Ben know that I would not or could not take over should he collapse on board. I labored under the mistaken notion that if he knew that I was incompetent, he would not sail unless he felt well enough. It became a not-so-subtle tug-of-war between us as his health became more precarious over the years. Looking back, it was not very smart on my part since accidents can happen on board to anyone at any time, and it would have served me well to have practiced my skills. Deep down, I knew that I could do it but wished myself into believing that it would not happen if I insisted on being helpless.

The joys of sailing far outweighed these undercurrents of disagreement. I was strictly a fair-weather sailor, though actually quite exhilarated the few times when the weather turned suddenly and the going got a little rough. Then Ben was in his element. Like other physicists, he was an excellent sailor, understanding the laws of wind and waves better than most laymen. His suntanned body, his laughing face, gray hair blowing in the wind, all surrounded by blue, form an image still dear to me.

Hawaii

The sound of ocean waves surrounds my being, envelops me in living, breathing tranquility. Hypnotic as a trance, a mantra of an orderly universe full of wonder, promise, and certainty that wave will follow wave.

The beach in Hawaii—shade of palm trees, stretches of sand, wave upon wave of foaming sea. All worries gone, all stuff of dailyness forgotten; reality is in the waves, the limitless expanse of blue and green and white. I feel it in my being, this rhythm of the sea, the power of nature, soothing and invigorating.

Later, I shall venture into this ocean. I will trust my body to its strong embrace. I will swim and float with the ocean's rhythm, taste salt upon my lips. I will feel my own strength within and upon the water. I will venture into the deep unknown but only as far as fear permits. Staying close to shore, swimming alongside the beach, mindful of my limits, yet feeling limitless, exhilarated, and finally at one with water, sky, and land.

Years later I sit at home, upset about the news, the war, the hunger, the cruelty of humans. My body is tense and anxious. This will not do. I know how I can find a bit of calm relief. I call to mind the sun-drenched beach, the sound of waves, the shade of palms, the warm air on bare skin. Yes, Hawaii is still with me, soothing, healing, and gloriously beautiful.

Our Last Decade Together

Come, my beloved
Be still, the light is gentle
Together we are one

The 1980s. Did I know that it would be our last decade together? Deep down, did I suspect? Ben's first heart attack was in 1962 and even before the second attack in 1984, I was in almost constant fear of his dying. He experienced frequent serious health crises: the prostate surgery that went wrong, the detached retina during a vacation in Ireland, the pacemaker that needed emergency replacement. The fear was always there, invading all decisions, all interactions, our intimacy, and our distances.

The 1980s was also a time of creativity and drive for me, the blossoming of my career, the fruition of the work that I had started so late in life. I organized and spoke at professional conferences. I wrote and edited. I felt and exercised my power in my work. I loved the networking, the emerging cross-mentoring with other women, the long-distance relationships, the excitement of sharing and developing ideas that felt new to us, the best of what's been called the women's movement.

It was a balancing act of major proportions. I felt powerful in my work and my writing, and powerless in the face of Ben's illnesses. Powerless but present and deeply hurting with him, for him, and for myself. I often felt pulled apart, like the time when Ben's recovery from heart surgery coincided with a professional conference. I missed the conference, stayed with him and tended to his needs. To say that I was torn between two roles is too simplistic and ignores the profound elements of love and connection that exist in a successful, caring, long-term marriage.

We both lived life to the fullest in those years, my life, his life, our life together, we wanted it all. He continued to be immersed in his research, writing grant proposals, new papers. He spent summer days on or about his beloved sailboat, and winter months out of the cold. We sailed together, traveled together, and visited our children's growing families. The attempt to balance our needs, our mutual and individual desires, often created tensions. We fought, we argued, and were more intensely close and intimate than ever.

We went through the ordeal of taking stock financially, estate planning, and tackling the legal issues. My fears involved not only the fear of losing my life partner, but also the fear of managing the finances on my own. I obsessed about wanting Ben to make a list of assets, instructions about the care of the boat, the house, and his books. And he resisted. That's not how he wanted to spend his time. I wanted things spelled out, he did not. What did he want done with his precious books, should I survive him? He didn't care. "I won't be there," he said.

Ben died in March 1990. My adjustment to widowhood was slow and painful. It was several months before I was able to return to work. Listening to the pain of others would have been impossible. My practice had dwindled because of long interruptions, and I preferred to keep it small. I felt a strong urge to take care of my own needs for connection and companionship, to spend more time with friends, other widows, and women of my own age.

Having found laughter by your side
The lightness of a day well spent
Seen enough quiet lakes for now
Walked miles of every season side by side
Known well the bitter tug of mine and thine
When sharing does not fill the empty space
Lived with the fear of loss and death
When reaching far too high for simple grace
    Being a little wiser now

For Ben

Still grieving.
This subterranean grief
Resists abbreviation.
Silently subconscious
In years lived alone

Days of fun and laughter
Joys and celebrations,
Days of sadness,
Funerals, losses,
Without you.

Grief suddenly emerges
When pleasure is intense
Or sorrow overpowering
When wish to share
Meets only void.

Tears dry in silent sobbing
Dreams bring back
Lost joys, lost touch,
Lost years entwined in love

Johnathon, Kaya Benjamin

For Johnathon

My tears dried long ago, the pain has dulled, but sadness fills my heart when I think of you. You were so full of life, brimming over with love and energy, with longings yet unnamed and unfulfilled. So much had not been said, so much was yet to be experienced when you died in 1996, at the age of twenty-five.

When you were born in 1971, Grandpa Ben and I were on sabbatic leave in La Jolla. We laughed, we cried, we took the day off to celebrate. Knowing that a child was on the way had not prepared us for the rush of emotions at becoming grandparents and welcoming you as the first member of a new generation. A few weeks later we were able to visit and share our joy with your parents. Hyam and Judy were so young and in love, they doted on this firstborn son. In one of those deeply felt intergenerational moments, Hyam was moved to say, "Watching Dad hold Johnathon, I realized how he must have looked when he held me and loved me as a baby."

You were a sweet and sensitive child, too sensitive perhaps. We adored you and delighted in spending time with you when you were a toddler, and later during your annual visits to our summer home. We marveled at your joyful break dancing routines, your appetite for fun and food. When Grandpa Ben took you sailing, however, your distaste of structure and discipline got in the way; you came home in tears with Grandpa equally frustrated. You were easily hurt, quickly angered; we tried to understand and humor you through some of your mood swings. You wrote beautiful poetry and we encouraged you to hone your writing talent. You were with me in Florida when Grandpa Ben died. You consoled me, reached out to rub my back, stayed close, and grieved with me. I felt your love.

Your own son, Kaya Benjamin, was born in March 1992, just two years after Ben's death. I felt his birth as a healing sign of life's renewal, and it eased my sorrow at Ben's death.

The next four years were tumultuous. You and Ea did a great job of parenting, but your growing attraction to drugs and trips to rock concerts created major problems and interruptions to your fathering and to your college life. We all worried about you. I wonder when you started using drugs. You were quite open about it. We had a conversation, you and I, in which you stated your strong belief that the drug culture would cause all humans to love each other and would lead to peace. You easily shrugged off my argument about the obvious dangers.

Then came that fateful October day. You had been ill, your throat was very sore. To ease the pain, you shared a dose of heroin with a friend; when he woke up, you did not. Your death left all of us with a bottomless void, an ache that has never been completely healed.

Your son, Kaya, was four years old. During your funeral, the little fellow picked up a lovely fallen leaf, walked to the open grave, and solemnly dropped it on your casket. The sadness did not leave his face for many years.

My Heart Keeps Growing

Never too full my aging heart
Room for more joy, love, easy laughter,
Sadness, pain, and sorrow.
Filled to the brim with love received,
Shared, given,
Lives touched, held,
Merged, and intertwined

Each death invades my heart entire
With presence of the one I loved,
Absence of our sharing.
Week by week,
Month by month,
Grief becomes memory.

Years go by
My heart gets fuller yet
Not breaking though it would
Feeling the void of lives long gone
The gift of lives that touched my own
Some old enough to go in peace
Others too young to die but dead

Room in this tired old heart for more
More loves, more deaths,
More life itself
So rich, so full.

S Is for Siegel

Siegel. Three pages of them in my address book. When I ordered my wedding invitations, so long ago, the printer said, "So you're choosing a name that's easier to say." From Josefowitz to Siegel, easier to say indeed! Easier to live with? Whatever. By now it's who I am. Mrs. Siegel.

No, I did not become simpler by taking on my husband's surname. Not simpler by far. Richer, yes, in many ways; more complicated perhaps; fuller, for sure, even in girth and possibly in mirth.

So Siegel it is and has become. I even say at times, "That's a Siegelish thing to do or say," and most Siegels know what that means. Yes, pages of them, the multiplying Siegels: the sons and daughter, the ones who have married them, even when divorced, still in my address book; the granddaughters and grandson, frequently changing their addresses and phone numbers as they start out on their separate paths; and now the fourth generation, great-grandsons to delight the heart. Then there are cousins, nephews, nieces, second cousins once-removed, all sharing not only a very common name, but sharing a sense of belonging, of being connected to each other. All recognizing, or looking for, or imagining some common threads in our behaviors, our attitudes. An instant affinity, stronger than that of strangers, even at first meeting.

We are not a clan, we Siegels, far flung and numerous. Some have been in my life for over sixty years, are dear to me, have shared loved ones, have shared memories. Some have died; some are with me still. Others have suddenly appeared, bringing a son or daughter to Ithaca College or Cornell, and we have formed new bonds. They have come into my home and quickly spied the Chanukah menorah that Ben brought with him from his home in Superior, Wisconsin. Delightedly they recognized it as identical to their own cherished heirloom from midwestern ancestors. This single ritual object embodies a shared family history, a multigenerational connection among people who did not know each other an hour ago.

They were part of American history, these Jewish settlers in Superior, Wisconsin; Duluth, Minnesota;

Fargo, North Dakota, arriving before the turn of the century, in the late 1890s, joining other mostly Northern European Swedes and Finns in settling new towns in distant regions. It is a heritage I have adopted through marriage and that I have helped pass on to my children and their children. Yes, I have become a Siegel wholeheartedly, just as much as I am still a Josefowitz with European roots.

When I started to write professionally, I needed to reintroduce my maiden name to assert my full identity. In my publications, I am known as Rachel Josefowitz Siegel. It is my way of letting people know the part of me that is harder to spell and to pronounce; the foreign-born, European, Jewish self who has become a full-fledged Jewish American Siegel.

Ben, Charles, Rachel

Our Firstborn

Two years into our marriage, I gave birth to our first child. It was a cold, snowy January day when Ben drove us from our rented house in Cambridge, across the Charles River, and deposited me into a private room at the Boston Lying-in Hospital, famous as the best and most advanced maternity center in the United States. I was young and as ignorant about babies and childbirth as most mothers of my generation.

The little fellow was not only our firstborn but also the first grandchild in both families. As such, he was duly admired and fussed over by the whole *mishpochah*. We named him Charles Ellis, after my uncle Charles Josefowitz and Ben's uncle Ellis Siegel and my grandfather Rav Eliahu Dov Shur; his Hebrew name is Yehezkel Eliahu. At first we called him Chazkale or Chazkel, Yiddish for Yehezkel. Then my sisters decided he needed a more American label. They started calling him Butchy. These nicknames did not last. Throughout his school years it became Charles, and later Charlie. So much for names, which seem to have been an obsession in our family.

Ben and I had read Gesell, the only book about parenting that was available at the time. It offered a blueprint of early childhood development that often gave us unrealistic expectations and did little to imbue me with self-confidence about this daunting new role of mothering. We muddled along, without much know-how, and learned by doing. After the first somewhat difficult weeks, he began to thrive and enjoyed all the attention given to an only child. He had us all to himself, as was his God-given right.

When the time came, we prepared him for the arrival of another baby, or so we thought. During my ten days at the hospital, he learned that I would bring home a baby brother, and he was full of anticipation. The day arrived. When we brought Barry home, Charles was quite fascinated by this helpless little bundle. After a few minutes he looked puzzled and asked, "Where are his mommy and daddy?" Having a brother was okay, but sharing his parents was an entirely different story. One day, a few weeks later, while I was nursing the baby, I became aware that Charles was awfully quiet. I started looking for him, found him on our big bed, his shirt pulled up, nursing his teddy bear.

He often lived up to his role of oldest child and older brother. When Hurricane Hazel hit Ithaca in 1954, Charlie was all of eight years old. Ben was away, the kids and I were home alone. We had no heat, no electricity. Charles rose to the occasion. He consulted with me, thinking through where best to place the *yahrzeit* candle overnight so that we would all feel safe and cozy without setting the house on fire. He made sure the young ones were tucked in and earnestly announced that I should call him if I needed him.

He was a serious and thoughtful child who loved books, first having them read to him and then reciting them by heart before he could read the words. Reading and telling stories are still among his favorite occupations.

His fascination with acting and directing was apparent in his early years when he would come home from seeing a movie and reenact the whole show, complete with sound effects. Theater has continued to be his passion, and he often conveys his enthusiasm and broad knowledge with detailed accounts of his current activities in that field. I listen, sometimes impatiently, but always with a sense of wonder at what has become of this firstborn son who, at the age of two, dressed in his short pants sailor suit, marched around in circles to records of classical music.

Now Charlie is in his sixties and I am in my eighties. I believe he still likes his role of eldest son. He watches over me, anticipates my needs, takes care of me when needed. He has become my computer guru, talking me through new procedures over the phone with great patience. We see each other once or twice a year, sometimes with his beloved family, often alone. We are not always in agreement and have learned to deal with that. At other times we trust each other fully. Our short trips back to the airport, alone in the car after a Vancouver visit, turn into moments of intimacy when we share some worries and speak our love.

Charlie's First Day of School

Every year in early September, when a brisk morning makes me feel that summer is nearly over, the cold snap brings back a vivid memory, tinged with nostalgia and a sense of shortcomings as a mother. I was all of twenty-six years old when Charlie started kindergarten, on the day that Ruth was born.

I remember that morning, the chill in the house, deciding that a hot breakfast was called for. I made oatmeal for Charlie and Barry. I was filled with anxiety over Charlie's first school day, bundled him up in long corduroy pants and his new fall jacket. Would that extra clothing protect him from the outside world, keep him safe and warm during his first foray away from home?

Off he went, and the day got warmer and warmer. By noon, when the poor child trekked home for lunch, it was a hot, late-summer day and Charlie arrived sweating and red cheeked, almost in tears. I had failed him, hoped it would not mar his school experience forever. I had committed the motherly sin of overprotection, had made that first school day more difficult for him. Would he be scarred for life?

Chelly

She is an early morning person, gets up at six or seven, even on not-working days. By 8:30 a.m., when she gets on the new Vancouver Skytrain, she has had her coffee. She has gathered last night's cups, books, and scattered newspapers, emptied the dishwasher, set out breakfast for her husband, taken out the garbage, watered the plants, and left a note on the kitchen counter for Charlie: "Don't forget to pick up milk and dinner rolls." She's out the door quietly; the only trace of her early rising is the odor of strong coffee that permeates the apartment.

She loves clothes, Chelly does, and has a flair for elegant dressing. Goes to work in a smart, tailored suit and shoes to die for. Mostly black, gray, and shades of beige and brown, though lately she has taken to a touch of color. No dowdy librarian here in flat walking shoes, not your old-fashioned stereotype.

Her quiet, unassuming, orderly presence sets the tone as head librarian of the Vancouver Art Gallery Library. Here too she exercises the vast knowledge, efficiency, and competence with which she runs her life and home. She has surrounded herself with equally pleasant coworkers and a bevy of volunteers, some of whom have found a new life purpose in her library.

Her people skills remain unsung, unmentioned. Unsung is perhaps not the right word for Chelly, for she has been recognized by her colleagues in the Art Librarian Association and has been entrusted with international leadership positions. At home, however, she seldom talks about her work or her accomplishments, unless she is asked. She does confide in Charlie when it comes to the internal politics of her workplace. Chelly is, of course, never without a book. When on vacation, when she visits me, the smell of coffee wafts early into my bedroom, and I find her on the terrace or in the living room, book in hand, a cup of coffee nearby. It is a good time for an intimate visit before the bustle of the day.

She is also an imaginative homemaker, decorating and redecorating her home with her own hands. When she redid the tiny guest bathroom on the ground floor of the old house, she chose a wallpaper portraying shelves of old books. Her guests could now peruse these virtual volumes while sitting on the throne.

Chelly is technically my daughter-in-law, but I think of her more as a daughter and friend than an in-law. I love her dearly. She shows affection and deep love in acts of kindness and generosity of deed and spirit, not overt effusiveness. To some, she may appear quite reserved, but that impression soon dissipates. When she comes to my home, she takes over the kitchen in her most noninvasive yet thoroughly matter-of-fact manner, producing gourmet meals with the same apparent lack of effort that goes into all her activities.

Charlie appears to be the dominant figure in their marriage, but she's no pushover. She follows his lead—spoils him, you might say—and does it wholeheartedly. Yet she manages, quietly, to meet her own needs and preferences as well. They are both devotees of theater and quiz shows; they enjoy each other's voluminous fund of trivia, of entertainment lore, and literary references. A true librarian, and a thoroughly up-to-date one, she uses the Internet as an extension of her library, quickly finding the answer for nearly every query.

He made a good choice, Charlie did, when he brought Chelly into our lives.

The Dinner Table

Three old friends   *Good food, good talk*
At first son's table   *Laughter*
Remembering   *Friends reconnect*

How many hours around the dinner table? How many meals, snacks, festivities? How many fights, heated words, hurt feelings? How many acts of love and acts of defiance? How many memories and unmemorable occasions?

Last week's dinner at Charlie's table was memorable. Chelly is a superb hostess of the old school. She had set the big round table with ultimate good taste and a touch of whimsy, using elegantly simple white plates and colorful linen napkins on a dark brown paisley cloth. Serving spoons, wine and seltzer, salad bowl, all waiting on the side table nearby.

It was for me the perfect ending to a lovely reunion day with Marion and Bev, my two old college friends. The three of us arrived in time for a refreshing drink before dinner, with assorted olives and a vegetable dip straight from the local Vancouver farmer's market. Hot and tired, we settled into the comfort of the cool, welcoming living room. I looked at the dear faces, known for sixty years, more wrinkled than last year, our bodies slightly more bent, our shoes less stylish and more supportive, our hearts and minds bubbling over with the joy of reconnecting.

To table we went. It was Friday night. Charles recited the blessing over the wine, and we all blessed the homemade challah. We fell silent for a moment, filled with the warmth of our togetherness and a surge of memories. Bev was the first to speak. Listening to Charlie, she had been reminded of Friday night dinners with Ben making *kiddush*. We launched into memory time, as Chelly quietly served the cold fruit soup that I had learned to make from Mutti so many years ago. The wild rice was Granny Siegel's recipe, each grain fluffy and fully opened, as it is served in Wisconsin and Minnesota where the rice used to be harvested by Native Americans.

Charlie talked about his burgeoning interest in collecting family stories. We shared our frustrations, our sense of loss about no longer being able to ask our loved ones about their early lives. Lost memories, lost heritage, lost family lore.

"Tell me," said Charlie, "tell me what you know." He was the first to tell what he had learned from his recent visit to Sam's house, sitting at Sam's dinner table.

"No, no," I chimed in, "that's not how it was, that's not what I was told, that's not how I remember it." Too bad we can't just Google the real story behind the many myths. But does it matter? Why not pass on both versions of the truth? What matters more is the sense of shared history, even if somewhat distorted by each teller's memory sieve.

Bev and Marion had been roommates at Simmons. I had lived on the same sixth floor of the then-brand-new Evans Hall. We had been witness to each other's growing up and our wartime romances, and now we were each widowed after long and happy marriages. Now again, as our children grow into midlife, we bear witness to each other's pains and joys. All this around the dinner table.

Barry & Ruth

Barry's Communications

He calls me on his cell phone from the car. We start with the usual safe openers, "How are you?" and "What's new?" I need to establish the absence of crisis in his life, the well-being of each of his children and grandchildren. Only then do we begin to chat, to share bits of news, ideas, tentative hopes and plans, the kind of talk that makes us feel close and connected over the miles.

When he was a toddler, Barry used language in his own quirky way. He had a tendency to take words literally. One summer morning when I asked him what he would like for breakfast, he replied, "Booze," and repeated the word when I looked puzzled. I finally said, "Show me," and he pointed to the fresh blueberries on the table. I got it. He had assumed that the "berry" part of "blueberry" signified his own name, Barry, so asked for "blues" in his own pronunciation. Another time, when he was about four, I told the children that I was going to a Hadassah board meeting. As I was putting on my coat, he came running after me, trailing his toy ironing board, as he was sure I would need it at the "board" meeting.

We were not always good at figuring him out, Ben and I. We had a hard time interpreting his speech and body language, his seemingly mysterious, cryptic phrases. We tried our best and showed our love in many ways, but sometimes we just missed the mark, or thought we did, and those instances have left me with a trace of guilt. Does he remember it that way? Probably not.

We know each other better now, he and I. We've had our ups and downs, real sorrows and many delights. We have been there for each other through his divorce and the tragedy of his son Johnathon's sudden death, and through my late-life illnesses. He is better able to express himself, and I have improved my listening skills, can better hear his words, his moods, his way of saying and not saying what is in his heart. Our miscommunications are mostly in the past.

When Barry was born, my father, who was dying, wanted me to name him after his own father, Solomon. Much as I wanted not to displease Papa, I could not burden the child with such a heavy name. We settled on Hyam, after Ben's uncle Hyam, and Dov for my maternal grandfather, the distinguished rabbi Eliahu Dov Shur. Our circuitous thinking led us to call him by his middle name, which by translating Dov, Hebrew for "bear," to the Yiddish Berel, became Americanized into Barry, a name that would not cause teasing in the schoolyard, we thought. So he became Hyam Barry, and we called him Barry throughout his childhood.

As an adult, he began calling himself Hyam, pronouncing it "Chaim" with the guttural Hebrew *ch*. But who am I to speak of names? My own name Rachel has been through numerous permutations of linguistic pronunciations.

Hyam has been a single dad for many years and has become an active grandpa, doing more than the usual share of grandparenting. Upon approaching his sixtieth birthday, he had a hard time deciding whether to celebrate, or endure, or ignore this milestone. He is an avid tennis player, sailor, and lover of the outdoors.

He chose, after some research and personal inquiries, to trek the heights of Nepal with a local guide and explore one of India's most beautiful beaches. Alone for six weeks, he met other travelers, took local trains and buses, explored the countryside, and enjoyed himself immensely. He kept in touch with us by iPod, sending meaningful accounts of his impressions.

He is no longer the misunderstood and inarticulate son of early years. I am no longer the frustrated mother trying to figure out his puzzling messages. We have both come to hear the love in our communications.

A Quiet Evening

It had been a beautiful day, September 13, 2009, in Plainfield, Vermont. Hyam and I had attended the wedding of my friends Nicola Morris and Barbara Johnson, in the meadow of their new home. The state of Vermont having legalized gay marriage on September 1, Nicky and Barbara were one of the first couples to formalize their thirty-year union.

When it was time for speechifying, Hyam surprised me by speaking up. Usually shy and reluctant to be heard in public, he expressed his good wishes to the newlyweds.

He went on, with great feeling, to speak of his pride at his own state of Vermont, for overcoming this aspect of discrimination against gays and making this celebration possible. My eyes teared up with motherly pride.

Now it was evening. Hyam and I settled in to our bed-and-breakfast suite, complete with its own living room and small library. We spied a large, worn volume of old *Saturday Evening Post* essays. Intrigued, we started reading to each other.

I remembered the times, years ago, when Hyam, then called Barry, sat at the kitchen counter with me at the end of the day, while he ate his customary nighttime snack of corn flakes. This ritual was often followed by reading him a bedtime story.

And so it was that night. No corn flakes, but the same intimacy, the same deep connection, being together without the hullabaloo of other family members and ordinary tasks. It was a rare moment, charged with emotion.

Seder Night 2008

As usual, the family had driven five hours from Vermont to Grandmother's house. This year, as in previous years, Hyam had tried to teach the youngest child, his grandson, to recite the ritual four questions in Hebrew by singing them to him during the trip. But five-year-old Ajna had refused to listen or to sing along. Excitement ran high as they tumbled over each other into Great-Grandma Shel's new retirement cottage, hugs and kisses and joyous laughter all around.

At table, it was time for the four questions, beginning with "Why is this night different?" Ajna was sitting next to Grandma Shel. She whispered to him. Would he try it if she led the way? He agreed. Slowly she started, *"Mah nishtano haleila haze?"* The child responded, repeating the ancient chant, word for word, in deep concentration. Question followed question to the fourth and final one.

Awed silence filled the room as four generations witnessed this precious moment of love and continuity.

Ruth

She was a hairless baby for many months, this little girl, born on her brother's first day in kindergarten. She arrived promptly, two hours after I had served the family dinner, and just before the doctor had rushed in from his late office hours. Doing it her way, even at birth.

Then, when she was able to sit alone in her infant table, she insisted on feeding herself. With utmost concentration, she picked up a glob of ice cream in her little hand, placed it on her spoon, and brought it to her mouth. and did it again and again while we watched in amazement.

Doing it early, and doing it herself, seemed to be her motto. Being a girl with two older brothers was both a challenge and an advantage. The boys always said that she was so cute, she got away with everything, and it was often true. On the other hand, she felt the frustrations of not being able or allowed to do what they could do, not only because they were older, but also because they were boys.

Ben and I were determined to encourage our children's creativity and development in every way, but we modeled and taught traditional gender roles without being aware of doing so. While we let the boys play with dolls when they were toddlers, we were not as quick to get a chemistry set for Ruth. We didn't even hear her ask for it, which she later told us that she had. Household tasks and Jewish rituals were gender specific as well, and Ruth was prone to resist and to rebel. No longer baby bald, by now she had a full head of black curly hair, and she insisted on washing it herself while still very young.

In nursery school at Cornell, the director predicted that Ruthie would become a teacher or a lawyer because she talked so much. Both predictions eventually came true. She earned advanced degrees in both fields, and wavered back and forth for years before combining her two vocations, finally teaching school law, her current occupation.

Ruth's Visit

Happiness is
Quiet of the night
Peace in my soul

She's visiting again, my grown-up, adult daughter, now middle-aged, still full of hopes and energy for things that may or may not happen.

She's here, more like me every year in voice and looks, and also more herself, with her own taste and preferences, her own extensive fund of knowledge and experiences. She is attuned to my moods, anticipates my needs, finishes my sentences. Our roles are reversed at times, almost. I'm still her mom. She fixes a loose screw on the guest room door, cooks a delicious fat-free dinner, solves a computer glitch, buys perch on sale and makes it taste delicious. She teaches me how to cook with salsa.

We hang out without words much of the time, and then we talk, confide, air out some worries, count our blessings. I watch TV with her, just to be near, watch shows I don't usually bother with. We giggle when her cat and my dog avoid each other, eyeing each other with a mixture of curiosity and apprehension.

She stays long enough for us to relax, do our separate things, the routine tasks that each of us needs to do. She's on her computer and I on mine. She is not into the Ithaca things that Charles and Barry like to do for old times' sake. Ice cream at Purity, dinner at Joe's? No, not with her. She'd rather cook at home, see her Ithaca friends, meet my Kendal friends. She does not care for the newer things that Tommy, Brenda, and the grandkids like to do—the Science Museum, the Paleontology Museum, Farmers Market.

Shopping together, which we used to do, is now too hard on my hip and back. I send her out alone with my credit card. "Get yourself some gloves for Chanukah. See what else tempts you, and please return these shoes to Bon Ton while you're there."

We say good night. Was something left unsaid? I don't remember. Say my love? I do that. Say please stay, move to Ithaca, get old with me? I've said that, too. We've talked about it honestly, no need to say it again. She has her own good reasons.

No matter how long she stays, it's over much too soon. Things I meant to do, to say, get pushed aside, not by her, but by my wish to be fully there with her, without agenda.

She spends an evening or two with childhood friends. She does my errands, makes healthy salads, buys avocados and sings their praise, and wonder of wonders, she even makes her own bed every morning, no longer the messy teenage kid I knew.

Eighty Years of Blessings, Year 2004

Eighty years of living, laughing, weeping, worrying, wondering. Eighty years of growing, in width and depth, in spurts and in slow motion. Eighty, hurrah! I'm eighty today! I've made it this far.

Time to count the blessings—the unbelievable multiplication of family members and loved ones. How could all this have come to pass just because Ben and I loved each other? In our passionate, joyful union, we were soon blessed with two sons, Charles and Barry, and a daughter, Ruth, a new generation. And wonder of wonders, as they have grown up, each has matured into a mensch; each one unique with strikingly different personalities, and each a loving, generous, and responsible human being.

Years go by, teenagers grow up, and oh so soon, voilà! A third generation. Our very first grandchild, Johnathon, is born in Brattleboro, then his sister, Brenda, and their brother, Tommy. Meantime in Vancouver we welcome Sarah and her sister Anna. Then Mathew comes into Ruthie's life. They say that counting your children and grandchildren is akin to courting the evil eye. The angel of death might hear you and be tempted to subtract. Who is counting?

Yet death comes suddenly with excruciating pain, leaving a permanent gap, a dull ache never to be completely healed. Our beloved Johnathon gone in youthful prime. He was our first and oldest grandson, He leaves behind his four-year-old son, my first great-grandson, Kaya Benjamin. The child grows up, the sadness slowly, slowly leaves his beautiful eyes.

Ben gone, Johnathon gone. Will I learn to live with such deep losses? The dark years, how many? Yet even then, in darkest times, in sorrow, more blessings come my way, more joys. As time goes on, I feel myself as one again, one among two brothers, two sisters, one daughter, and two sons. Don't ask me to count the grandchildren. I hesitate but name them out of love. Sarah, Anna, and Brenda are now tall, talented, beautiful, and smart; Tommy a competent, kind, and handsome man. Mathew has returned, after a stint with his birth family.

Six years later, I am now eighty-six, the year is 2010, the *mishpochah* keeps growing. Tommy has married Sarah Brown, their sons, Rylan Sidney and Maxwell Harpur, have come into the world. Sarah has married Alan Tse. Kaya is now nineteen, Ajna is eight. Mathew has earned his practical nursing license. My heart again is filled with deepest gratitude as I count not children, not grandchildren, nor great-grandchildren, but the joys and blessings of my long life.

Surrounded by this lively brood and so much *naches*, my heart is fuller than I could imagine. What I count are the miracles of life repeated, renewed, love multiplied. My life abounds with pleasures and accomplishments, while challenges and disappointments fade. All this and I am still alive, still able to take it all in, still able to count every day and every minute.

MORE LOVED ONES:
PARENTS AND SIBLINGS

Rav Eliahu Dov Shur   Rochel Gitel Shur

Anikst
Josefowitz Family,
Sonia, Velvel,
Solomon, Frada,
Chaya, cousin ?,
Fruma, Zachar,
Gregory, Charles

Berlin
Josefowitz
Family,
Papa, Sam,
Rose, David,
Rachel,
Mutti,
Grandfather
Shur

Siegel Family, Superior
Gita, Ben, Pauline,
Aaron

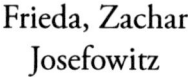

Pauline, Aaron Siegel

Frieda, Zachar
Josefowitz

Three sisters: Rose,
Rachel, Fenny, 1990

David, Fenny, Rachel,
Sam, Rose, Geneva
2011

Hillary, President
Clinton, Rachel, White
House, 1999

Rachel, Hillary,
Ruth, my home,
1999

Anna   Brenda, Ajna

Tommy, Sarah, Rylan, Max
Tommy/Sarah Brown's
Wedding, 2011

Anna, Chelly,
Charles, Alan,
Sarah, Rachel,
Sarah, Rylan,
Tommy, Ajna,
Brenda, Hyam
Barry, Maxwell
Sarah/Alan Tse's
Wedding 2011

Genealogy: A Labor of Love

In my desk drawer is a thick folder labeled "Genealogy."
After Ben died, there were so many things I still wanted
to ask him. Not just "Where did you put the keys to
the boat?" or "How do you think we should reinvest
the CD that has matured?" There were things that I
wanted to know and be able to tell my children when
they asked. Things like how many cousins you actually
have and what their names are. And who was that uncle
I never met, and so on?

Since I could no longer ask him, and because his
sister Gita, the last living member of his clan, was no
longer able to keep her thoughts together, I determined
that what I could do was write down what I knew of
our two families. I felt a strong obligation to trace the
genealogy of our far-flung and numerous *mishpochahs*.

Why? I ask myself. Why? What is this urge to be
the keeper of family lore, to make sure that it becomes

accessible to future generations? There are surely answers to that question, psychological, sociological, historical answers. Whatever. The fact is that the project occupied me, heart and soul, for quite some time. I started out recording all the living relatives, going back as far as our collective memories could take us. I discovered that I was actually the only one in the family who had any records at all.

My chart goes back to my father's great-great-grandfather and my mother's earliest ancestors. One of my Shur cousins traced Mutti's rabbinical family back through the centuries to the illustrious Rabbi Solomon Luria, 1510-1573, a descendant of Rashi, 1040-1105. The *Encyclopedia Judaica* mentions a seventeenth-century Polish tax collector named Josefowitz, who converted to Catholicism in order to keep his position. His brothers remained Jews and moved to Lithuania. We have no proof but have liked to believe that these were our ancestors. My chart does not go back that far. Ben's chart goes back to his mother's great-grandfather, our common ancestor.

In the process of asking distant cousins about their families, I found that others had done some research into immigration records and Lithuanian census reports. We began to communicate. The father of a non-Jewish, third cousin-in-law sent me a copy of the Lithuanian census of 1900 that listed my father's family. Some of the names were unfamiliar in their Russian version, though I was able to recognize their derivation. The researcher and I began to disagree. He was convinced that the written record must be more accurate than the oral recollections of an old lady like me. I am quite sure, of course, that I am right. One argument was about my great-great-grandfather, whose name I know as Dov. That name means "bear" in Hebrew and translates as "Berel" in Yiddish. The written record referred to Bera, which could easily be a transliteration of the Yiddish, and all other markers being accurate, was the Dov that I had heard referred to by my father.

I came across more distorted versions of our family history, mainly concerning our immigration to the United States in 1939, during the time of Hitler. Our journey must have fired the imagination of some American relatives. Cousin Helene in California insists that when we arrived in New York, Papa gave Mutti's diamond ring away to the wife of a potential business contact as a gesture of our wealth, even though, according to Helene, the ring was the only asset we had been able to rescue. Not true.

My fascination with family lore is shared with my brother Sam, who has more recently put much energy into assembling facts and stories. He has absorbed my genealogy chart into his far more extensive records, which have been researched and elaborated by Anna, my youngest granddaughter.

Our family keeps growing, and our common history is now recorded. I feel that the work that Sam and I have done in tracing our genealogy, with help from Anna and others, has reinforced our personal connections with known and unknown relatives in Europe, America, Africa, Australia, and the Middle East. Furthermore, I feel a richer sense of my own identity within the now-named generations of my *mishpochah*.

Mutti

My mother had been a midwife before she was married. Her love of babies was evident as she approached an infant, with complete confidence and professional demeanor. At such times, her whole body proclaimed the pleasure of her expertise.

Her knowledge of babies, however, did not continue into the toddler stage, and even less into adolescence. Oh, she did continue to love us dearly, but mostly she didn't have a clue about how to steer us into the customs and expectations of the unfamiliar lands of our migrations. She knew all about food and nutrition and poured her love into feeding and overfeeding us, comforting us with sweets when we cried or were upset. She also conveyed her wisdom and self-assurance in nursing us through the usual childhood illnesses and the occasional broken bone. Unlike my mother-in-law, she did not panic when confronted with a sick child or an ailing husband.

She was an immigrant mother, coming out of a *rebbe's* house in a Lithuanian *shtetl*. She had, however, defied her father by leaving home for a two-year hospital training in midwifery. She proudly told me of studying human anatomy when women of her generation were, and were supposed to be, quite ignorant about their own bodies. One of her early recollections was that of delivering a baby in a household so poor that there was nothing clean to wrap the newborn baby in. Mutti took off her own petticoat and tore it up for swaddling clothes.

She was not a typical product of Jewish *shtetl* life, yet never fully at home in the affluent ways of Western Europe and even less in the New World of America. She learned a smattering of the new languages but less of the customs. She did not understand the child-rearing ways of our Swiss environment when we lived in Lausanne and then in Zürich. But Mutti put great value on our education, hired tutors when needed, music teachers at early ages, and exposed us to outdoor sports. She did not, however, speak the language of our teachers, or spoke it haltingly. She had no contact with the parents of our classmates; her social life was confined to a few Jewish families. Later, in America, when it came to choosing colleges and guiding us through the system, neither she nor my father were at all informed, though Papa had definite opinions.

Like other immigrant children, we absorbed the new culture more quickly than our parents did. It is only much later, an immigrant mother myself, but educated in the United States, that I saw how involved other parents were in the selection of colleges, and how involved they were in PTAs, school boards, and teacher conferences.

Yes, my mother loved babies with utter confidence and self-assurance. As we grew up, she loved us still with food and warmth and old-fashioned admonitions. When her grandchildren came into the world, her early mothering skills and pleasure showed up again, as she physically handled my babies and their babies with loving delight.

In her old age, when all of us had come to terms with our international adjustments, Mutti exuded unconditional love without relinquishing her habit of honest criticism. Living in Israel among Yiddish-speaking neighbors with similar backgrounds, she had no trouble fitting in. She continued to be a steady source of calm and innate wisdom, generously advising and welcoming her grandchildren as well as near and distant cousins. Young people loved and trusted her.

The Work of Mutti's Hands

My mother of blessed memory spent her days knitting and crocheting. Her hands were never idle. When I was little, she hooked rugs. The rugs have disappeared. I remember a small one in blues and gold, perhaps three-by-five feet, that I wish I still had. She made many beautiful things. Her finest, most delicate work was a set of white, crocheted place mats with a long center runner. I treasure the runner and adorn my dining table with it on special occasions. Sometimes I just feel the need to have the work of her hands on my bare table for a while. At other times I have placed it on top of a white tablecloth to make the table look more festive.

When Mutti's eyesight began to dim and her fingers became less nimble, she knitted. Oh, she knitted way before that. I remember knitted bathing suits when we were very little, then beautiful sweaters. These are collected in my memory.

When she lived with Ben and me on Forest Drive, late in her eighties, she would get up at seven every morning, get her own breakfast, and settle into her chair by the picture window to catch as much light as possible. There she started her daily work, knitting baby blankets for each grandchild, a custom that I tried to follow, mine never as perfect as hers. She also assembled knitted squares into full-size blankets.

When she could no longer see the knitted rows, she turned to crocheting blankets and throws, from single bed to king-size. She prided herself on finishing the work with no yarn left over. I still have the dark brown king-sized blanket and the two burnt-orange ones for the twin guest beds. The one I use most often is the off-white throw, so nice and cozy for an afternoon nap. More blankets grace every one of her children's houses, as well as some of her grandchildren's.

She made triangular stoles as special gifts for her loved ones, relatives and friends. She liked bright colors and would take orders for favorite colors as well. As her eyesight faded, she could no longer see the darker shades, but did not stop working.

The last of her crocheted gifts was a baby blanket for her granddaughter Nina's daughter. It came out crooked and she cried with anger and frustration, no longer able to count the stitches with her fingers or see where she had stopped the work.

Over the years I have occasionally given one of her scarves, her knitted hats, her stoles, to one of my granddaughters. Sarah wears the wooly hat that is nearly falling apart. Brenda treasures a white stole and Anna one of the scarves. I often feel Mutti's love and the comfort of her presence in the work of her diligent hands.

The Frieda Shur
Josefowitz Collection

In 1984, I made a gift of books by and about Jewish women to the Cornell University Hillel Library. The gift was in memory of my mother, Frieda Shur Josefowitz, known to all who loved her as Mutti. She died in Jerusalem in 1983, peacefully in the ninety-second year of her life.

She was not a reader, so why did I give books? Let me try to explain. She had enormous respect for education. Not only had she completed high school when other Jewish girls in Lithuanian *shtetls* were rarely even admitted to public schools, she also completed a two-year training in midwifery. In order to do this, she had to defy her father, the distinguished Rabbi Eliahu Dov Shur, and move to Vilnius, where she first roomed with relatives who also disapproved of her endeavor. Her mother, Rochel Gitel Lurie Shur, a practical woman, was the only one who gave the young woman her blessings and support. Mutti earned her way by working extra hours at the training hospital. In later years she talked to me with pride of her own stubbornness and determination, which kept her going. She also liked to recount the memories of being picked up by horse and buggy in the middle of the night to help a woman through labor in an isolated farmhouse, or the time she delivered a breech birth before the doctor arrived, which was against the rules but saved the infant's life.

She married her childhood sweetheart, Zachar Pincus Josefowitz, again defying her father. My father, an agnostic, was not religious enough for the rabbi's daughter. On the other hand, she was not rich enough for her mother-in-law. They pulled it off. They were both rebels and strong willed. They moved from Lithuania to Russia, then back to Lithuania with a growing family. On to Germany, and later Switzerland, they finally settled in New York City. Mutti spoke Yiddish, Russian, German, some French, and some English. After my father's death, she joined my youngest sister, Fenny, in Jerusalem, where at last she felt at home again.

A woman of modest needs herself, she never got quite used to being rich. My father did become a capitalist along the way. She was enormously generous, giving of herself and her means. She did not care for most organized charity or organized religion, but gave when and where she saw the need. The need she recognized most often was that of education, and she helped many a niece, nephew, and other young relative through school, often putting them up in her home. She had a warm and accepting rapport with young people and was able to communicate with them in her own mixture of languages.

So why not books for young people in a university setting? It does make sense after all.

My mother and I did not always agree. What drew us together was, of course, the *mishpochah*, the family, our shared history, and our deep love for each other. Beyond that, it was also a concern for the lives of women, the health of women, and a deep respect for a woman's right to make her own reproductive choices.

I hoped that my gift would link generations of Cornell Jewish women to the richness of their own heritage by reading the writings of other women.

Papa: Mythical and Human

Papa has become a mythical figure, larger than life. He died at the age of fifty-seven, shortly after Hyam Barry was born. This birth and death are inevitably associated in my memory. The joy of Barry's early months was sadly overshadowed by my grief.

Charlie remembers being brought into Papa's sickroom in the family apartment on Central Park West and placed on the bed beside him, having been warned to be very quiet, a difficult and intimidating task for a three-year-old. Papa clearly enjoyed this special moment with his first grandchild. He also got to hold Barry, the new baby, for a few minutes of intense emotion. I stood by, all of twenty-three years old, presenting my sons to him in a gesture full of symbolism, filled with a mixture of grief, joy, and confusion.

Papa died in January 1948, sixty-plus years ago. The colorful legend of his life that each of us tells and remembers has been elaborated and embellished through our individual prisms. His legacy lives on in various versions, leaving his imprint on numerous members of our extended *mishpochah.*

In legend, he looms large and powerful and smart. He was indeed smart enough to repeatedly move our family out of harm's way in those tumultuous years of the Russian Revolution, Lithuanian famine, and German anti-Semitism. He was smart enough, through his business dealings, to amass and manage a fortune big enough to finance these upheavals and keep us all in comfort, if not downright luxury. He was indeed powerful enough to cajole, instruct, convince, and succeed in getting every member of the clan out of Europe before Hitler's Final Solution could reach them, and smart enough to know who to bribe and when not to.

In stature, Papa was a short man, rotund, and certainly not athletic. He traveled a lot on business, always with his little black leather attaché case full of medicines and his soft travel pillow. When he was home, Mutti watched his diet, made fresh yogurt and cottage cheese for him, home-ground chicken burgers, and of course, chicken soup.

Both powerful and vulnerable is how I remember him. His loud booming voice could put fear into us all. He never hit us, but his tongue could be sharp in disapproval, and once, but only once, he slapped my face. I had embarrassed him when he was entertaining some important business acquaintances, by coming home late and disheveled from a Girl Scout outing.

My fear of upsetting him was fueled by an unnamed knowledge of both his power and his neediness. Mutti's quiet admonitions had even more effect than his own voice. "Papa is sleeping, or working, resting, eating, don't disturb him," or "Don't upset your father." As a young man, in order to avoid being conscripted into the Czar's anti-Semitic army, he swallowed some digitalis, thus self-inflicting a heart condition that plagued him the rest of his life. He suffered from angina but eventually died of cancer.

The tales of his clever and successful financial dealings live on, along with stories of outwitting

Russian dignitaries in order to get a distant uncle out of Siberia. He was charming and gregarious, and he enjoyed entertaining those around him with a glass of vodka and a humorous anecdote.

But what comes to my mind when I think of him is the feeling in my little hand, taking long walks with him along the Quay d'Ouchy, my hand in his until I was too old for such comforting protective touch, and too proud. He would talk; he loved to talk, as we walked past the manicured flowerbeds along the water's edge. Interspersed with his stories would come a loud fart, usually when we had reached an area free of other strolling families. This was invariably followed by "*Ahh, a mechayah*," a Yiddish expression indicating the kind of pleasure you get out of stretching your limbs, or sinking into a warm bath, or as in this case, freeing yourself of accumulated gases. His occasionally unrestrained behavior and lusty laughter at off-color jokes were also part of his legacy. In fact, I too have been known to acknowledge my relief at the loud blast of my own gases in the privacy of my home. My words echo his, "*A mechayah*," I'll say, or an Americanized version: "There's more room outside than in."

When I think of Papa, it is this combination of his very human frailties and honest physicality, combined with his almost superhuman qualities that warms my heart and makes me feel proud. He loved his family, he liked good food, he liked to laugh, to be irreverent, and to see through and beyond false premises, and so do I.

Rachel, Fenny

My Kid Sister

Fire, fire, fire, fire—the phonograph record went round and round, the sound of sirens in the background. I liked playing it over and over. I remember the thrill, the frisson of fear within the sure knowledge that it was just a song, a recording. I was eleven, a big girl, but my kid sister, Fenny, was only six, a little girl, and she was truly scared. She hated that record; she dreaded it. She would cover her ears and tremble, the sound frightened her so much.

It didn't take long for me to learn that all I had to do was threaten her with the record or chant, "Fire, fire, fire . . ." and she would give in to my demands. I soon figured out, brat that I was, that I could use it to control her. I was mean—or was it just a means of overcoming my own frustration when Fenny was stubborn? All I had to do was put the record on and she would stop what she was doing and agree to anything I asked of her. Oh, the easy tyranny of older sisters. And then I could console her, make nice.

Now, to be fair, dear Fenny was at times insufferable, though I can't for the life of me remember what she did that drove me up the wall. What was it that pushed my buttons and made me want to stop her, control her? I only remember the feeling of frustration that she occasionally evoked in me, the sense of powerlessness, and yes, I admit, the ensuing glee with which I welcomed my power over her.

Now that we are both old women, living far apart, seeing each other only once or twice a year, we often reminisce together. More often than not, our memories do not match. We remember different events, and we remember events differently. I have long been haunted by my guilt over the *fire, fire, fire* incidents. I have regretted my cruelty. One day, when we were feeling especially close, I apologized to Fenny.

Guess what? To my surprise, she found nothing to forgive, she had no memory of these encounters.

David's Violin, Volta Strasse, Zürich

Full notes rise,
Fall, repeat
Sing

Deep low sounds
Echo melody
Vibrato

Little girl listens
Big brother plays
His violin

The sound of David's violin fills the room. Every afternoon after school I listen for David's arrival and rush to the music room. I know that before doing anything else, he will pick up his beloved violin. Sometimes he wanders from room to room, playing, never stopping, and I trail after him, my big brother. He is playing Bach, but I don't know that. The music is so much who David is, so much an essential part of him. It feels to me as if it is his own improvisation. Only much later, when I listen to the same Bach partita, do I realize that David was not improvising.

The music fills me with love and a sense of peace. David is the sound, and the sound is David. When I remember us in the music room, I discern no other sounds in the big house. I know that he is not playing for me, perhaps he is not even aware of my presence, my listening. He is one with his violin. His beloved instrument is an extension of himself.

Many years later I open the door to the patio one evening to let the dog out. I hear the silence, a moment only of complete silence in the stillness of the dark. That moment takes my breath away. I am reminded of David's violin and transported to the same sense of oneness, of awe, and of beauty. My heart is full of joy and of belonging.

Now he hums music	*Old woman*
Remembers not when or where	*Older brother*
Only his violin	*Dry tears*

Sam's Visit, 2007

Morning fog, brother visits
Deep joy and sadness.
Old together

My brother Sam came to visit. One night only from his home in Lausanne, and on his way to a medical check-up at the Mayo Clinic.

My brother Sam, the keeper of family histories, self-styled patriarch, generous supporter, thoughtful helper; the financier, shrewd businessman, serious art collector. My lonely brother Sam. Divorced from his first wife, now widowed from the love of his life, he travels, he visits, he tries to cut the loneliness.

We sat at the kitchen table all morning. He showed me his recent photos of our sister Rose, ninety years old, without the make-up, looking more and more like Mutti. We talked of David, who now lives in the moment only, bad news forgotten as soon as heard.

Sam had photos of Aniksht, the *shtetl* in Lithuania where he was born, as it looks today. He told tragically disturbing stories of his recent trip to Lithuania and his futile search for remnants of what had been the thriving Jewish community of our parents and grandparents.

We did not weep.

When it came time, we meandered slowly to the Kendal dining room, he with his cane, taking photos of my new environment. He told my friends that he had come to check up on his little sister.

He came, he left; our hearts filled with each other's presence.

Sam, Rachel, in Playschool, Berlin

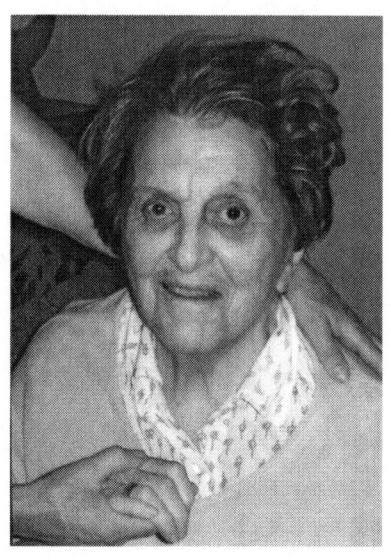

Rose

Sam is traveling in India on his yearly trip. His house in Lausanne is still elegant and grand, but somewhat past its prime. This house holds memories of beautiful parties, festive lunches on the terrace, laughing children, and Calif, the German shepherd. It has been a house of love and joy, of family and laughter. It is still a house of love and family, the deep love of old age, of illness, loss, and grief. A house of caring without the joy, where laughter is a rare intrusion.

Life does go on. The caged birds sing, the cook prepares delicious meals and fabulous desserts. The broken toilet gets fixed, the rooms get aired and vacuumed, and at the center, in her little room, my sister Rose is cared for. Marie, her caregiver, gently coaxes her out of bed to bathe and dress her. She brings her downstairs to share a meal with us. Marie cuts up her food, tells her what is on her plate, hands her the spoon. We talk; that is, I talk to Rose. I start the conversation, try topics that can engage and stimulate. Rose does respond, but she does not initiate. She is still sharp, even offering touches of humor and selected memories. She makes an effort, for effort is required. She is interested and interesting, still full of knowledge about art and language. She was a poet and a painter, but now cannot see enough or care enough to even choose what she will wear each day.

We got her a Scrabble board with extra-large letters that she can see. She loves it. We play after dinner, and Rose makes great words but cannot see well enough to place the tiles on the board. I help her, and we play each other's hands as we always have, for she likes the game more than the winning, though she always won. Now we can barely finish, we stop after an hour or so. I talk about how to spend our last two days. So soon, she says, and bursts out crying.

That last morning she is up early, wants to get out of bed, wants to have breakfast with us. I indulge in my last croissant with Swiss butter.

We sit together, do the family parting ritual, a moment of well-wishing: "May we come together again in good health." We cry, a few gentle tears. My deeper sorrow travels home with me.

Rose, Rachel

Blue Is Our Color

Blue is my color. Blue for me is the color of hope and calm. I am surrounded by blue clothes, walls, drapes, sheets, and shower curtains. When the sky is blue my mood shifts into joy and wonder at the beauty of my universe. When I glimpse a stretch of blue lake or ocean, I feel energized. I love blue. I need blue in my life.

Blue is also Rose's color. She taught me about blue for the walls of our first married home. My big sister Rose knows more about colors than I ever will, she is a painter and can remember the exact tint of a blue horizon and reproduce it with her brush. She could, that is, years ago, before her blindness set in. Now she can no longer tell green from blue, know my face, or see the color of her clothes.

I land in Geneva for my annual family visit. It is a rainy afternoon in March 2009. The sky not blue, but gray, the lake nearly blue-black, the mountains hidden under a sea of clouds. We speed along the superhighway to Lausanne, not along the Route du Lac of childhood memories. No longer do we meander through curved roads and old-time villages. No, we rush along; so many vineyards now replaced by industrial buildings, motels, and fast-food establishments. Only occasionally do I catch sight of the sturdy homes that used to dot the terraced vineyards. The beloved landscape of my childhood has been transformed by seventy years of industrial development, population growth, and urbanization.

"She is better," they keep saying. "Can you see how much better she is?" True, Rose is better. She does get out of bed these days, even joined me for breakfast on the first morning of my visit. She looks better; her helper/companion is good at applying subtle make-up.

Rose is in better spirits, is more awake, and has more energy than she did a year ago when I last saw her. She is now proud to announce that she is ninety-three, born in 1916, not 1917, as she would have had us believe in earlier years. She calmly tells me that she does not have much longer, perhaps a year or two, possibly less, so her doctor has said. Last year she was neither proud nor calm about her age and her disabilities.

She clings to me. "Rochale," she keeps calling me, my Yiddish name. She wants to touch my face, hold my hand, and is deeply happy to be near me. Last year, though she did cling, her need to get back to bed was stronger than her wish to savor my visit. I too am glad to be with her. My tears well up but do not surface as I see her world so diminished, her helplessness, her struggle to bring the spoon to her mouth, the carefully cut-up spoonful prepared by Marie, her helper.

I converse with her, bring up pleasant memories, tell her good news about my children, my grandchildren. She wants to know, she listens eagerly but can no longer figure out relationships. Over and over, "Who is Tommy? Do I know him?" and "Who has the new baby? I can't figure it out," she says with a resigned shrug. And then she lapses into forgetfulness and starts over: "Did you say there is a new baby? Barry's grandson?"

The sky turned blue on my third day, blue sky, blue lake, and the French Alps sprinkled with a layer of fresh snow, just as I remembered them.

FRIENDS

Milton &
Mary Konvitz,
Rabbi Morris &
Helen Goldfarb,
Hannah Aber,
Rachel & Ben

Marion Poliakoff,
Rachel, Beverly Unger

Roz Feinstein,
Carol Skinner,
Nina Miller,
Rachel, Mickey
Goldstein

Dear Helen

I miss you. Not every day, but intensely when I do. Ours was such an easy, unexamined friendship. Both young with our young families, our busy lives. It took about a year for me to overcome the sense of you as a *rebbetzin*, a rabbi's wife, a respected and slightly older woman who set standards of behavior I tried to emulate.

I remember the moment in the parking lot in back of the old Rothschild building, when my reserve broke down. You had not yet learned to drive. I was trying to get into the only parking space available when someone beat me to it. I don't remember what expletive came out of my mouth, but I do remember my feelings of consternation and embarrassment. Swearing in front of the rabbi's wife! You burst out laughing, of course, and we giggled together. The ice was broken. We were equals now. I still admired and respected you but no longer felt intimidated.

You were my first best friend in adulthood. We talked every day, shared errands, cared for each other's children. We cooked together, bought matching *milchige* silver-plate at the Oneida factory outlet store, and borrowed teaspoons from each other for large parties. On New Year's Eve we partied together with our husbands and the Konvitzes. It didn't take much bubbly for each of us to break out in uncontrollable giggles. But when it came to our attempts at playing bridge, I couldn't stand dear Morris's putdowns—his "father knows best" attitude—and we stopped playing.

The year we spent in Jerusalem, you sent us your sixteen-year-old Judy a month before your own arrival. We loved her as our own. We found you a great apartment just down Balfour Street, only a block away. Came Pesach time, your landlord entrusted you with access to their Pesach dishes, but your kitchen had only two burners. Our kitchen was not kosher, but we had a regular oven—unheard of in Israel in 1960.

We made Seder together. Our outing to the Mechaneh Yehuda market was a memorable experience. The pre–*yom tov* crowd of noisy housewives, children jostling underfoot, the tantalizing smells, the shouts of vendors. It took us all morning to buy the one huge pot that would serve both families. We shopped and bargained together. I became annoyed at your indecisiveness, and you resisted my impulse to get on with it. Good friends have squabbles, and this was one of them. But we got over it, schlepped our bundles home. Again, I had the car and was the driver.

Now came the really fun part, also a tour de force of orchestration. The new pot went from house to house; I cooked the soup in my kitchen, you made gefilte fish in yours. The pot came back to me for *tzimmes*. Not all the groceries from our shopping spree had ended up in the right household. The kids were home and we enlisted them, running from one kitchen to the other. Ruth carried onions back and forth, Barry delivered the carving knife where needed. The shared new pot went back and forth, the matzo meal made several trips. I wonder what the neighbors thought about this relay race up and down Balfour Street. Talk about laughter! It was like a Borscht-belt comedy, and I still giggle when I think of it.

The sad parts came years later, when we consoled each other, confided our large and small worries as our children lived through the anxieties of the Vietnam War. I had a hysterectomy and you had a miscarriage. We were there for each other.

When I went back to graduate school, we drifted apart ever so slightly. You did not share or quite

understand my newly found ambition, my emerging
feminist awareness. I did not share your resistance to
change. We still cared, spoke daily. By now, we were
family, inseparable, with different perspectives on some
issues, but with a bond that would forever be with us.

Then, slowly, you drifted into an unknown,
unknowing world of your very own. It was after your
mother died. You forgot when and where we would
meet; you misplaced food and other items. You were
depressed, being aware for a while that something was
wrong. It took perhaps a year or two before I allowed
myself to realize that your brain was now impaired. The
dreaded word "Alzheimer's" became reality. I grieved
for you, for Morris, and your children. I grieved our
friendship. When you died, it was as if you had died
long before.

I miss you, Helen, and I still miss our friendship.
I cherish the years of youthful bonding, plotting,
planning, working together on Hadassah projects, and
confiding the small stuff every day. Sharing holidays,
comparing recipes. It's been a while since I've used your
brownie recipe, since I no longer bake. Last Pesach I
cooked a brisket, lining the pan with a sliced onion and
a small can of tomato sauce, just as you used to do. I
thought of you, and it was good.

Old Friends

Happiness is hugging a good friend
In pain or in pleasure
Or just because

When I visit Ben's grave in Lakeview Cemetery, I find him among our dear old friends, the friends who shared our young parenting years. For a brief instant I feel like joining them, I want to stay with those who had been young with me. Here, in this beautiful, quiet cemetery, I have more old friends and close friends than I have outside in the land of the living. And still more in distant cemeteries: Helen and Morris Goldfarb in Hawaii, Mary and Milton Konvitz in New Jersey, Hannah Aber in Toronto. Tears come to my eyes.

It's been such a long time since they left my life by distance, by Alzheimer's, and by death. I am now the lone survivor of the three couples who were family to each other, who raised children together, played together, laughed together, and grew up together. It's been a long time now, over twenty years, that I have lived without them. At first, when each moved away, there were phone calls, rare visits, e-mails. Then came the news of their decline, their deaths, and my lone grief.

The only friends of that generation who are still very much alive are Mim and Harold Scheraga, who now live at Kendal as I do, and Chippy (Charlotte Fogel), who lives too far for easy visits.

The old friends who are gone live on in cherished memories, appear occasionally in my dreams, and sometimes make me cry. To say that I miss them is too simplistic, for their lives have touched mine deeply. To say that they are with me in spirit sounds trite, yet it is true. Their love of life, their generosity, their little foibles, the sound of their voices, are all part of me, they have given color to the landscape of my life. Their children, now middle-aged, feel like family and hold a very special place in my heart.

My earliest friends go back to college years at Simmons, where Bev Kerness Unger and Marion Secunda Poliakoff lived on my floor. We knew each other before getting married, witnessed our wartime dates and courtships. In later years, we have attended class reunions together and managed to see each other almost yearly.

Now I am blessed with later generations of good friends, newer old friends. In the 1970s, when I went back to graduate school and immersed myself in my new profession, I met new people, made new friends. This more recent cohort dates back some thirty, forty years by now.

Nina Miller is my dearest friend of that generation. She and her husband George became my next-door neighbors on Spruce Lane after Ben died. She saw me through my widowhood and the sudden loss of my grandson Johnathon. And I was there for her when George died three years ago. She has housed my children and grandchildren during happy times of family gatherings. Nina is also a member of what started as a consultation group, along with Roz Feinstein, Carol Skinner, and Mickey Goldstein, who died much too soon. We have consulted each other professionally and have continued to meet as friends all these years. We trust each other and deeply respect each other's work. We talk about our inward journeys and matters more mundane. We enjoy a unique kind of ease and intimacy, having lived through our midlife adaptations, losses, discoveries, and spurts of personal growth. We have come to know each other's adult children and grandchildren, have listened to our bragging and kvetching about our families. We have become old friends.

These women are younger than I, and I cherish the intergenerational aspect of our friendship, yet I realize that their favorite tunes are those of my children's teenage years, their feminist awakening came at an earlier stage of their family life, early enough to affect the way they raised their kids. And there are times, more recently, when I need more help, more downtime than they do. My arthritic joints and damaged heart keep me from joining their activities. I can no longer keep up when we take even a short walk or contemplate a trip together.

Sheila Stone, also a colleague, has a special place in my heart. Having dated Hyam for several years, she is my could-have-been daughter-in-law and has remained like family to me. Tony Pane, a former colleague, is my regular lunchtime companion. We are fond of each other and meet every two weeks at DeWitt Café. His wisdom and experience with adolescents and their families has often helped me understand the dynamics of my own family. I tend to forget that he is the same age as my children.

Mary Salton and I go back some fifteen years. We were first drawn together by the loneliness of widowhood and by our immigrant past, having both grown up in Switzerland. We often lapse into French, German, or Yiddish, as I do with my European family, where speaking at least three languages is the norm. We sometimes act like sisters, comfortable and caring; we check in daily once a day or more, sharing our thoughts and the trivia of the moment.

Nicky and Barbara came into my life the year Ben died, while Nicky was grieving the loss of her mother. Ours is an intimacy of Friday night dinners, of Jewish talk and woman talk. We eat and laugh together, sometimes uproariously. My rabbi, Scott Glass, and his wife, Sharon, have seen me through the worst of times. We have a very special relationship. Our mutual admiration and friendship mean a great deal to me.

At Kendal, new friendships and acquaintances abound through common interests and affinities. Dinners turn into what Rose Bethe calls "real conversations" about politics, ethics, science, and the human condition. We keep each other informed and exchange personal as well as global concerns.

These current friendships, new and old, are no less dear to me than older ones; they keep me grounded, connected, and involved in life outside myself. Without my friends today and all the yesterdays, I would feel empty and most desolate.

Lists

I love making lists. Making a list helps me organize my thoughts, get centered. I'm not really an orderly person, but I feel better, safer, when things are in order. Making a list helps me feel less overwhelmed. What really feels good is crossing items off the list when the deed is done.

Often I make a list at the end of the day about things to do tomorrow; then I can go to bed without carrying all that stuff in my head. When I wake up, I enjoy the feeling of efficiency as I do the chores that have been listed and cross them off with a flourish, instead of rummaging in my crowded brain for what it was that I wanted or needed to do. At the end of the day, I indulge in a sense of accomplishment as I look at the items that I've crossed off, instead of wallowing in thoughts of "What did I do all day?" Just look at that list, all done!

Then there are grocery lists, which hopefully will make their way into my purse before I go shopping. These grow at odd moments, at their own pace, as I jot down each item whenever it occurs to me.

This morning I started making a shopping list that helped me deal with grief and confusion. My friend Mickey died last night and although I was expecting her passing, I found myself in tears and shock. Mickey and I have been friends and colleagues for over thirty years.

My way of coping with death and its finality is to jump into "What can I do" mode. What needs to be done? Mickey's family is coming in from far away; they will need food in the house. So that's where the list comes in. A grocery list, breakfast foods and comfort foods.

Death makes me feel powerless. Part of me wants to just let go, go back to bed, cover my head, and weep. Usually, however, I choose the alternative: I pull myself together, I take control over what needs doing. I make a list.

HEIRLOOMS AND RECIPES

Tzimmes

A small number of favorite dishes have survived the changing culinary habits of my life. One of these signature recipes is my *tzimmes*. I cook it often when I entertain or when I bring a dish to pass.

Tzimmes is the word for a slow-cooked mixture, perhaps derived from the Yiddish word *zermischt*, or the German *gemischt*, which means mixed. It is often a dish served on Jewish holidays or on the Sabbath, when observant Jews, being forbidden to do the work of cooking on Holy Days, have developed foods that improve by staying warm on the back of the stove throughout the following day.

Mutti made tzimmes with carrots, potatoes, onions, and brisket. Needless to say, it was mouthwatering, calorie-rich, and delicious. She served it on holidays, flavored with the additional spice of family festivity.

When I got married, I was determined to learn to make tzimmes. My first attempt was modeled on Mutti's tzimmes, and I was quite pleased with the result. But Ben was used to *his* mother's tzimmes, and mine was nothing like it. He was kind and polite. I wanted so much to please him that I tried to find out how Mother Siegel made hers. Ben's recollections were vague. At his suggestion I switched to sweet potatoes (unknown in Eastern Europe), instead of white. That second attempt was still not quite right. Every week Ben remembered, or tried to remember, some other item. No onions, he said, and no brisket. Maybe his mother used chicken fat instead of meat; maybe she added turnips. No, she did not add prunes, as some recipes called for. By then I was researching in Jewish cookbooks as well as listening to Ben.

Some months into our new marriage, Ben's mother announced that she would come to visit. In anticipation, my mother arrived to give me a hand in making sure that my new mother-in-law would approve of my housekeeping. I was a young bride, all of twenty years old, and could use some pointers. Mutti, who was tall, rearranged our small kitchen. Since she seldom baked, she moved the baking flour to the top shelf, along with other rarely used objects and foods.

After Mutti left, Mother Siegel arrived, and immediately wanted to make herself useful. She was short, and since she liked to bake, the flour pomptly came off the top shelf.

I eagerly watched her make her tzimmes: sweet potatoes and carrots cooked in chicken broth. That's it. Cooked on top of the stove until done, then placed in a moderate oven in order to enhance the slow-cooked flavors and to absorb the broth. To say that she saved our marriage is an exaggeration, but she did defuse my growing sense of frustration and anger, which had come close to exploding.

Over the years, I have experimented further, taken ideas from friends and cookbooks. Often I add prunes and dried apricots, sometimes a bit of orange juice. I substitute vegetable broth for chicken broth. Some people love my tzimmes and ask for it on festive occasions; some pick out the prunes and prefer it without; others are just not into it.

One thing is sure. I always make too much and end up with leftovers that get more flavorful day by day. That too is part of the tradition, handed down over generations of both families.

Vanilla

Mutti's vanilla sauce was a childhood treat. The taste still lingers in my nose and on my tongue. My memory of it bubbling on the stove, its aroma permeating the house beyond the kitchen walls, continues to bring on a sense of euphoria and of well-being, pleasing to all the senses and to the soul.

I never got the recipe. I never even watched her make it. I do remember the satisfying odor, the visual pleasure when it appeared, smooth and golden on the dinner table. We poured it over stewed pears or fruit compote, and sometimes over cake. It always elicited deep sighs of complete satisfaction.

Nothing has ever tasted as delicious.

Tomatoes

Toe-may-toe or toe-mah-toe, the fruit is a source of varied pleasures and delicious memories, but I've never settled on its pronunciation.

Tomatoes for breakfast—what a treat, whether as a fruit or a vegetable. The best are the gorgeous large beefeaters that abound at the Farmers Market in August.

I think of my brother Sam, whose regular breakfast includes a whole tomato and a whole cucumber, both of which he slices at the table with appropriate anticipation and concentration. They must be fresh, out of someone's garden or off the farm. He eats them with cottage cheese, a slice of dry toast, and a cup of strong tea.

Sam goes to Saturday Market in Lausanne every week when he is there; he stops first at his favorite vendor. The two of them start with a personal conversation, greeting each other with sincere pleasure and exchanging news about this week's fruits and vegetables. Sam likes food and he will go to great lengths to bring home specialty foods from other countries. Thinks nothing of packing a large jug of New York maple syrup from Ithaca's Farmers Market in his luggage on his way home across the ocean. His visits from Switzerland always bring Swiss chocolates, of course.

Back to tomatoes. Unfortunately, the winter varieties are not as delicious, and Sam is seriously disappointed when his daily tomato does not come up to par. If it's not the best, it's not worth eating, he says. He is in tomato heaven when visiting our sister Fenny in Israel. There, no matter what the season, the hotel breakfast always includes fresh local tomatoes, cucumbers, and peppers.

In Paris, years ago, we learned to eat sliced tomatoes with sliced onion, a dash of vinegar, and sometimes a sprinkling of basil or chives over it all. In Israel we savored chopped tomato/cucumber salad with plenty of dill.

These dishes bring back succulent culinary memories and rich associations with distant places and special times.

Chelly, Ajna, Brenda, Boychik, canine friend

Ode to My Favorite Kitchen, 1992-2007

The ultimate recipe is making a kitchen: first came the planning, measuring, putting fantasy to paper, with the expert guidance of Martha Armstrong, my architect. Then came the building of it, the excitement and anxiety, pouring love and money into it, probably in equal parts. It was much harder than baking a pie. I needed a kitchen worthy of all recipes and all visitors, a kitchen to feed my senses and my moods. My kitchen on Spruce Lane was a study in light and warmth, a place of many delights. This, my favorite kitchen, is a place of memories, as many or more than any kitchen I've ever made my own.

Oak handles punctuate white cabinets, enough of them to hold the many dishes of a kosher household, including the now easily accessible Passover supplies. Drawers galore of various sizes for utensils, tools, dish towels, plastic ware, paper products, carving sets, matches, pills, and ill-assorted paraphernalia. The lower cabinets have room for vases, coffee pots, large pots and pans. Some are divided for large and small trays. Oh, what abundance.

Armenian tiles dot the walls with gentle creatures, birds, gazelles, the lion and the lamb together, circles, and flowers. These are souvenirs of the little shop in the Old City, that sunny afternoon during one of my Jerusalem visits. I chose them carefully, packed them among my clothes, and carried them home in my hand luggage. They brought me joy even before I had selected the deep-blue Corian countertop.

The wide cooking island divides the spacious expanse into a cool, efficient work space on one side and a cozy eating area where two oak cabinets are glass-enclosed. The space between them holds books and precious items such as my blue English teapot displayed on open shelves. The oak-framed kitchen table was a rare find the week before moving in. Its white tile top matches the wall tiles as if made for each other.

This is where I ate my breakfast, lunch, and dinner, usually alone, watching the news on the small television. I let my eyes wander to the collection of family photos on the counter, surrounded by objects of earlier days and years gone by. The large round stone mosaic of two birds, found on our first visit to Israel, is a copy of an ancient decoration above a doorway, executed by elders in a Haifa senior center. The ceramic bird plate came from a seaside kibbutz. We found the blue-and-white one in San Gimignano during our lovely trip to Florence. Marcia Polenberg's set of three small bells hangs nearby.

My little kitchen witch, brought home from Hungary, kept an unobtrusive vigil over pots and pans and souvenirs, keeping all safely balanced.

Past or present, I write as if I still lived and cooked, ate and breathed and daydreamed in this wondrous kitchen of mine, and I suppose I will continue to feel that way, though I have moved on. I have moved out, taking the memories, the witch, and my favorite objects with me.

The Spruce Lane kitchen still holds the joys of holiday preparations with granddaughters and grandsons cooking and baking, with children, dogs, and great-grandchildren underfoot. Popsicles out of the freezer in pudgy little hands, African violets thriving on the windowsill. Memories of a house full of laughter and surrounded by the warmth of family and friends, the lingering smells and visions of love and companionship in blue and white and sunshine.

Haiku Chain

Kitchen table
Food and solitaire
Plenty

Plenty books
Plenty years
Alive

Alive and well
Alive and kicking
How much longer

How much longer
Years of loving
Who knows

Who knows, how come, why?
Never-ending puzzles
Life

Life, she said
Heart breaking
Grieving

Haibun

I sit at my kitchen table, watch TV while eating breakfast, not quite ready for the day. I need more time to let thoughts wander. A game of solitaire and then my eyes drift to the row of family photos. They are all with me, my dear ones, so far away. Now I am satisfied. Food in my tummy. Food for the soul. More than enough. Plenty.

Chinese Teacups

I was eleven years old when we moved to Zürich in 1935, into a spacious and handsome house on the hill. My mother, a rabbi's daughter, had grown up in a Lithuanian *shtetl* (Jewish ghetto village), where the rabbi was paid in occasional gifts of eggs, potatoes, or firewood. Her family's modest home had been imbued with love of learning and pride in an ancestry of generations of rabbis. Now calmly managing a large and beautiful home in Switzerland, she was not yet comfortable with the customs and pretensions of "gracious living." She was a quick learner and did it well.

We had a small, intimate room off the living room, hardly ever used. The Chinese room, we called it. My memory is of red silk cushions and soft furniture, with shaded windows onto the garden. This is where Mutti entertained on rare occasions when she had tea with Mrs. Gutstein. Tea in the Chinese room, served on Chinese porcelain teacups, was perhaps the finest example of Mutti's transition into the newly affluent and elegant world of Western Europe. This is when she used the Chinese tea set. The round-bellied teapot with its matching sugar and creamer, the round porcelain cake platter, and the fine cups and saucers. She had special small spoons and silver sugar tongs that disappeared long ago. With me still, and rarely used but highly valued, are six cups, eight saucers, the teapot, and the creamer. The cake platter has a special place on top of the dining room buffet, a reminder of times gone by.

On a beautiful afternoon in late summer of 2005, I felt an overwhelming urge to drink tea out of those Chinese teacups. My friend Giorgi was working in the garden, tears streaming down her face due to a recent loss in her life. She needed a good cup of tea. Not just out of one of my best, most delicate mugs, but out of a china cup held on a china saucer. The elegance of Mutti's Chinese tea set made us both feel calmer.

It had been years since I had taken these precious, hand-painted, fragile cups out of their safe place in the cabinet behind the glass doors. I handled them gingerly, with great care and much love, for they are full of memories.

Now I use them more often. Sipping tea out of these fragile heirlooms, I imbibe a sense of continuity and well-being.

Grandmother's Candlesticks

How did I come by my grandmother's precious silver candlesticks? The truth is, I don't remember. Was it my mother who presented them to me? Or was it my Uncle Hy, my mother's brother, having no children of his own, who decided to pass on this family heirloom to me? Clearly, and without a doubt, I am the only one of my generation in my family who would make regular use of *Bubbe's* candlesticks, the only one who made Jewish traditions and rituals an important part of her life. And so it was, shortly after my marriage to a Jew more observant than I had been, that I received my candlesticks. My husband, Ben, is the one I thank for nurturing my then-dormant search into my Jewish heritage. Grandmother's candlesticks are emblems of this search and our commitment.

I never knew my maternal grandmother, Rochel Gitel Shur. She died shortly before my birth, and I am named after her. I know that she was a rabbi's daughter and a rabbi's wife. I imagine a woman of strength, for I know that against her husband's wishes, she supported her daughter Frieda's goal of becoming a professional midwife. Perhaps being named after her was significant in leading me into a fascination with her world, the world of Jewish ritual and Lithuanian *shtetl* customs. I like to think that it was through her and more directly through my own mother, Frieda Shur Josefowitz, that I inherited my own inclination toward feminism, activism, and a passionate involvement in the lives of women and the lives and history of Jews. True, my maternal role models would never have thought of themselves as feminists or activists. They would have called it *narrishkeit*, nonsense, but their actions have spoken loud and clear to me.

The candlesticks have taken me through a lifetime of Friday night and holiday observances. In the early days of marriage, I lit the candles in loving harmony with Ben's expectations of Jewish family life. Gradually the children filled our home, and elements of prayer became part of the family ritual. Our daughter, Ruth, learned to recite the blessings with me, and later the whole family joined in.

The children grew; they left home. I realized one day that I was no longer blessing the candles for them or for Ben. I was and had been doing this for myself. Lighting the candles on Friday nights gives a welcome rhythm to my week and a sense of connection with my past and future.

When the rumblings of feminism reached me in the early 1970s, I became aware of the limited role of women in Jewish life, the male God language, and the exclusion of women in so many important realms of religious and secular Jewish life. Now the lighting of Friday night candles became an assertion of my own emerging feminism. Not to negate or ignore the previous meanings of this act, but rather to enrich the ritual with yet another layer of cognitive and emotional significance.

Now that I live alone, my grandmother's candlesticks and my ritual use of them have become a link to my own memories as well. As I light the candles, I am often flooded with the warmth of family memories, the years of festive meals and dear ones around the table, the times of joy and intimacy.

SEASONS

Seasons

I have always loved the rhythms of life, the daily waking up from sleep, treasuring the half-awake, the change of light at dusk, the cooling breeze, the stillness of the lake, the glory of the setting sun.

I rely on the weekly change of pace, from busyness to relaxation. I hold dear the concept of the Sabbath, the weekly transitions from busyness to relaxation, from profane to holy and back to dailyness, to the tasks of living.

I mourn and celebrate the passing of each season, from grass to snow, from hot to cold, from light to dark, and in between. The years go by, season after season, with gradual maturing, school terms and graduations, first driver's license, first vote, new jobs, marriage, parenting, postparenting, moving, traveling, living in different countries, climates, languages, and getting old.

I suffer through and slowly heal from painful, sad transitions of illness, widowhood, and deaths too many. Have the forced transitions of my early life given me the strength and flexibility to take all seasons in my stride?

SPRING

Surprises every day

How soon

The lilacs

SUMMER

Garden flowers

House flowers

Running nose

AUTUMN

Branches dance

Leaves shimmer

Quiet moment

WINTER

Yesterday's snow hat

Now puddle

On slate table

Now Is the Time

Dreams of future   *Autumn leaves*
Become memories   *Glorious colors*
Of years past   *Gone*

Time to watch the leaves of autumn turning into a final burst of glory before falling to the ground. Gently they drift, a slow, mesmerizing dance of colors: gold, orange, red, and bits of green. Each leaf a separate thing of beauty, making its own journey down to earth and soil. Soon, moved in unison by wind and currents, they shrivel into crumbling shades of brown. Their end is near; they will be raked, discarded, mourned perhaps by just a few.

Like leaves, our bodies change. We too become more brittle; we may fall or not, in our own time, in our own manner. We plan, we worry, we write instructions, we wish to be well treated, not discarded at the end. With luck, good genes, and caring doctors, we continue to live fully, still giving love and pleasure to our dear ones, still taking in their gifts of care and their companionship.

Now is the time to rejoice in the beauties of late life, the wisdom of accumulated experience. Unlike the leaves of autumn, we humans do not show our late life colors on our sleeves, we keep our dance of memories inside ourselves. Our daily lives absorb new sights, new knowledge. Our memory banks are full and prone to slow retrieval; we absorb new facts at our own rate, make new connections. We each follow our own journey, in our own time. The loves and losses of long life feel bittersweet; we have few words to sing the fullness of our aging hearts.

Now is the time to be aware, awake, each day a special gift, each friend a precious asset to be cherished, each family moment to be fully relished and added to the store of feelings and deep joy. Now is the time to discard past injustices, small irritations, the clutter of the mind and heart. No need for balance sheets of our life's pleasures versus pains, but time, high time, to feel the present and the past in all their glory.

The hour is now. In childhood we looked forward to many years of adult life. We still look forward, now to a shorter span, treasuring each day, each human touch, each falling leaf, and every setting sun.

October

One night too hot
One night too cold
October

Shanah tovah wishes
Peace, health, love
More than words

Apples and honey
Raisin Challah
Sweet round year

Brilliant sunset, harvest moon
Year after year
Awesome wonder

To Every Thing There Is a Season

Doing nothing, how delicious. Doing nothing is my new vocation. It's been growing on me gradually, the enjoyment of quiet time, idle time, of minutes stretched to hours of being unproductive, even lazy. Lying in bed a few more minutes only to wake up an hour later. Playing a hand of solitaire that turns into thirty minutes. Puttering around the Internet in search of some unimportant chimera.

Some days I feel too lazy to water the plants or empty the dishwasher—what for? These things can wait, no need to do them now, maybe later, maybe tomorrow. Doing nothing, yet the heart keeps its own rhythmic beat, the mind stays active, the blood flows, the lungs breathe. The body is not doing nothing. The body, even tired and old and creaky, keeps me centered, alive.

Thoughts emerge; memories, daydreams, occasionally an insight. Then suddenly, a need, a wish to do something,

something specific. Call a friend, write a card, tackle a needed chore. Sort the mail, pay the bills, remember what I've been meaning to do. Doing nothing will run its course. To every thing there is a season. Doing and not doing take their own time.

WHIMSICAL NOTES

Alphabet Soup

S   is for start, for Sam, Siegel, and seagull, for the men I love.

L   is for love, luck, and lonely when loved ones are not with me.

M   is for Mutti, my mother, her memory, she and I.

I   is for island and intimacy, involvement and joy.

J   is for Josefowitz, of course, for brothers and sisters and cousins galore.

G   is for Grandma, that's me, and counting my blessings.

B   is for Ben, years of loving and fighting and fucking.

F   is for Fenny, my sister, and fun and her poems.

P   is for pleasure and pain, and playful ecstasy.

E   is for elephant, enormous, and envy turned into action.

A   is for always, for memories that stay with us.

U   is for undesirable, unethical, unwelcome, and odd obstacles.

O   is for other, not I, not me, not us, distant.

D   is for David and music, dementia and wonder.

W   is for women, wonderful, sisterhood, and revolution.

R   is for Rose, Rachel, and Ruth, a tradition of caring.

C   is for Charlie and Chelly, middle-aged, full of vigor.

V   is for volumes, virtues, and visits not taken.

T   is for tranquil and tempestuous, opposite notions.

N   is for nonsense, naughty, and staying in queue.

Q   is for questions and queries, from millions to zero.

Z   is for zits and zebras and the ending karma.

K   is for kvetch and Kunst and KKK, go to hell.

H   is for Hyam, for help and humor, the end, Hurray!

Numbers

My life is full of numbers. Some people think the daily number has to do with the lottery. Not on my scale! My weight, up and down, pounds or kilos, my blood pressure, up and down, too high, just right, even a bit low. That brings up the numbers of pills, morning pills, evening pills, pill bottles. The numbers go up or down. My age goes up, predictably, day by day, year by year, and my height comes down, less predictably.

When did I start counting pills, and pounds, and dress sizes? Time is numbered, life is numbered: twelve months, four seasons, 365 days, every year but leap year. When did human beings begin to think in numbers, begin to record numbers, in dots and scratches, with sticks and stones, on fingers and toes?

Numbers are useful. We think in numbers to make order out of chaos, to help us remember, to keep track of where we are going and where we have been, how far it is, how long it will take. We explain our world in numbers. We number streets and telephones, we number coins and dollar bills. We add, subtract, multiply, and divide. We have words for numbers beyond imagination. Large numbers: What's a trillion? Or tiny numbers: What's a submicron? What's one to the minus ten? What does it all mean?

Our scientists understand what it means, but do our economists or political leaders know what the numbers mean? Do they know the number for hunger or the number for soldiers killed? Do they know the true number for deficit and debt and really understand it? Numbers are useful, but they can also be confusing. They can be manipulated, they can tell the truth or hide the truth, and can reduce the truth.

Does counting our loved ones tell all there is to tell about them? Does counting blades of grass tell us the beauty of a meadow? Do the numbers and drops of water explain a river or an ocean? Does even the number of years we have lived tell who we are or the true measure of our lives?

We can play with numbers and enjoy the game. We can count numbers and learn something. We can ignore the numbers and get away with it, sometimes. We can obsess about numbers and get lost in them.

Without numbers where would we be? Can we imagine a world without numbers? How would we understand our fingers and our toes?

If

If I could start over, would I be a perfect mom? Would I always listen and understand, never lose my temper, succeed in nonsexist parenting? Would I always be consistent and in perfect harmony with Ben? Would our children grow up free of neuroses, emotionally stable, successful in every way, and have no reason to see a shrink or put the blame on me?

If I had a pony and no arthritis, would I ride through the forest, hair flying in the wind? If I were old but not creaky, would I climb the Swiss Alps again and ski down in virgin snow?

More Than a Broken Leg

I thought all I'd done was break a leg.
I didn't know there would be more involved, not
only pain.
My children came, nurtured and pampered me
I relished all that tender care,
Felt warm all over,
Healed deeper than one broken leg.

Yes

There have been times when I couldn't say yes and I couldn't say no. Caught in a strangling web of indecision, I dared not imagine what yes or no could mean. I could only get as far as "What would they think of me?" and "What if it's a mistake?" Now in old age, YES has become my motto.

YES to me and YES to you.
YES, not "yes but."
YES to life.
to no and if and maybe.
to now and later, or not at all.
to saying no and meaning it. No thank you, not this time.
to not yet, or just plain no.
YES to wavering, inconsistency, and hesitation.
to standing alone.

to decisiveness, rigidity, and stubbornness.

to love, friendship, and connection.

to hate and anger, fear and shame.

YES to the pain of loss, for it will pass.

to coping with disease and healing.

to tackling the uneasy.

to dropping the impossible.

to imperfections, yours and mine.

YES to differences and otherness.

to the misery of a dull day.

to the joy of sunshine.

to the pain of childbirth, smelly diapers, sleepless nights.

to the miracle of giving birth, the wonder and curiosity of endless questions.

YES to the pride and joy of nurturing each child into a mensch.

to the humdrum nitty-gritty of daily work.

to the fun of a job well done, to satisfaction and success.

to trial and error, mistakes and accidents.

to lessons learned or not learned.

YES to our bodies, the pleasure of our senses, our appetites for sex, for food and drink.

to interactions between young and old.

to old age, aches and pains and creaky joints.
to memory lapse and hearing loss.
YES to laughter that eases all discomforts.
to wisdom, clarity, intensity, and memories.
to seasons of the earth and seasons of our life.
to me and YES to you and YES to all of us.
to life and YES to death and to the magic of each day.

In My Next Life

In my next life I will arrive on time, no matter when I start.

I will wake up refreshed at 7:00 a.m. and enjoy a busy morning.

I will eat all I want without gaining weight.

I will hike valleys and mountains way into old age.

I will devour the Sunday *Times* before Monday morning.

I will laugh more and jump for joy.

I will always remember people's names.

I will find time to read more and more and more.

I will sing and join a choir.

I will learn Russian.

I will read and write Hebrew and Yiddish effortlessly.

I will be the firstborn child and not let anyone boss me around.

I will be a brilliant, famous writer.

I will be funny and never depressed.

I will live and love passionately.

I will never hurt anyone, knowingly or unknowingly.

I will make mistakes without feeling guilty.

I will know when to say "Enough" when enough is enough.

Never

I never climbed Mount Everest, not even Mont Blanc.

I never rode an elephant, went on safari, saw lions in the wild.

I never trekked the tundra, swam the Channel, kissed a kangaroo.

I never won a Nobel Prize, a Prix Goncourt, or earned a PhD.

I never wrote a novel, a concerto, or a children's song.

I never played mah-jongg, spoke Chinese, danced till dawn.

I never learned shorthand, speed typing, physics, or accounting.

I never understood what keeps the Internet alive.

I never changed a tire.

I never baked a decent pie.

But on the other hand:

I've never lost my sense of humor, wonder, awe, and sheer delight.

I've never lost my love of life.

I never have and never will.

Listen

Listen!

Can you hear my thoughts, my feelings? Can you hear the love over the Internet, over the phone? Can you hear how much I miss you? Listen to the old woman alone at home, waiting for the phone to ring, not daring to speak her loneliness, not wanting to burden you with her needs, not speaking out her heart to you. Listen carefully, listen to her wish to hear your love expressed again. Listen to love unspoken, yours and mine.

Things I Have Learned in Eighty Years

The time to love and speak my love is always now, not later.

The time to speak my anger is before it explodes, or never.

The time to speak my mind must be carefully chosen.

The time to learn is never over.

OLDER AND WISER

Old Is Not a Dirty Word

I did not wait to be old to wear purple, for I never thought of it as an old woman's color. I couldn't wait to be older when I was young—until I was sixty or so. Then, when others were horrified by the very word and fled from any mention of *old*, I embraced it. I claimed it early on, felt old and needed to deal with it. "Old is not a dirty word," I said. Yes, old is for purple and bright red to complement gray hair and paler skin. Old is for liberation, no need to prove myself any longer. Old is for being who I am, as I am, and reclaiming all that I have been and done. And now, twenty-seven years later, I am old-old, no longer midlife-old, but late-life-old. I am making friends with the next stage, the final stage. I wear purple even more.

I've always looked to the future with some pleasurable anticipation. Now, I take pleasure in the present. I look to the future with some unease, but also with a growing sense of calm as I face the unpredictability of late life and the nearness of death. Like every previous stage, this final stage of life is full of surprises, both good and less good, but far more enjoyable than I could have imagined it would be.

Collections and Transitions

Shredding papers
sorting memories

The time has come for another transition. A late-life move out of the house that I had built fourteen years ago and love dearly, into an attractive, attached cottage in a retirement community. It's been a complicated, challenging time full of intense feelings and realizations, a time of learning and growing, on the whole more exciting than stressful. It has certainly been less painful than I had anticipated. My life, this summer of 2007, has been dominated by downsizing my household belongings and parting with beloved objects.

The time has come to separate my worldly possessions, the cherished items I have collected over the years, into the ones I keep, the ones I give away, and the ones I recycle or throw away. Surprisingly, this has become a deeply satisfying process. Each of my children, grandchildren, and great-grandsons has carefully chosen the objects that hold meaning for them. Kaya, my oldest great-grandson, age fifteen, shyly asked for the Southwest weaving that hung in the upstairs hallway, and Ajna, age five, wanted to take care of the stuffed doggy that resided on one of the guest beds.

What is junk and what is precious? What is heirloom to be preserved and what has outlived its temporary purpose? What is important to me and what is meaningful to others? Which of my children would love and care for my mother's embroidered pillow covers? Who among them will make ritual use of my grandfather's kiddush cup? And most pertinent, what can I part with in joy instead of sorrow, for it gives me great pleasure to pass on these gifts of memory to those who will cherish them in their own way.

Recycling ordinary useful items gives me a different kind of satisfaction, as extra sheets, pots, pans, and dishes go to the Advocacy Center, Catholic Charities, or the Salvation Army. I once saw a stranger walk down the street in the beautiful wool jacket I had purchased in Stratford, England, and had later outgrown. It made me happy to see her wearing it in comfort.

Last week when I visited my grandson Tommy in his first home, I was thrilled to see the lovely Safed landscape that Ben and I had purchased on our first trip to Israel. The painting brought back memories of a hot summer day in the courtyard of the artist's studio and our enchantment with his work. Tommy will most likely remember the day I gave him this painting by Amitai. He will not associate it with the town of Safed or the enthusiasm of the artist who sold it to us. Parted from me but not forgotten, the objects are gone but not the memories. Now in the homes of loved ones, they take on a life of their own, create new memories.

Some collections are still with me. The Chanukah menorahs sit proudly on the special rosewood shelves in my now smaller living room. The *chanukiot*, as they are more accurately named, are not of a specific style or period; each has its own significance. The brass one came from Ben's family home in Superior, Wisconsin. The handsome silver alloy art nouveau specimen was designed and fabricated in the workshop of Hans Teppich in Jerusalem. It sits next to the nineteenth-century Moroccan silver oil menorah with dark blue velvet backing which we found in an antique shop across from the King David Hotel during the final week of our Jerusalem sabbatical year. There we also purchased the antique Italian brass one. Years later, Hyam gave us a playful pottery half-circle of old Jewish men with candles on their heads, then Ruth brought home a large and very delicate *chanukia* of colorful blown glass. I cannot part with these *chanukiot*; they will have to be claimed by others after I die.

I view my collections now as my life evidence, telling snippets from our travels, sketches of where I have been and what I have found meaningful and beautiful. I have always felt that my home, ours as a family and now mine alone, reflected who we were and who I am. My visible objects tell my story. Yes, this is who I am. I am the woman who loved and collected dishes for a kosher kitchen and opened her home to many guests. I am the woman whose taste in art was akin to that of her husband, who loved to shop for beautiful objects when traveling with him. I am the woman who needs to have photos of her large extended family on her bedroom entrance wall. I am also the woman who holds on to every object given to her by her children, her grandchildren, and her great-grandchildren, and who parts only sparingly with her mother's crocheted shawls and bedspreads. I am the old woman who wonders where it will all go when she is gone.

Home at Kendal

New house   *Photos everywhere*
new sheets   *babies grown, friends gone*
no lover   *love in frames*

In 2007 I moved into Kendal, a local retirement community. Kendal at Ithaca was started by a group of Cornell faculty and continues to attract residents who had been associated with the university, as well as other retirees. We enjoy one another's company, have interesting conversations around the dinner table and in various interest groups.

I feel at home now in my new home. The boxes are unpacked—well, nearly all of them, some two or three still hiding in the front hall closet. My favorite paintings and decorations are newly hung on pristine walls. The gallery of family portraits has found its rightful place in the bedroom entrance way. The Chanukah menorahs gleam in the living room on their transported rosewood shelves. My grandmother's silver candlesticks hold court next to Granny Siegel's brass ones. The African violets greet passersby from the kitchen windowsill.

I feel at home in this new home, well, most of the time. I'm getting used to my new bed and feel cozy and at peace, surrounded by familiar furniture. The headboard and night tables show signs of wear, of spills and scratches; the dressers, his and mine, are both filled with underwear, socks, scarves, sweaters, nightgowns, and a sachet of dried lavender, my favorite, soothing scent.

The walk-in closet feels a bit strange, some shelves higher than need be, my slacks too crowded on the lower one. Various unsorted treasures are still waiting to find their logical place and maybe never will. What is the extra dog mattress doing in that corner, and will I ever use that many pillows again?

When it comes to the bathroom, a miracle of downsizing amazes me. The contents of six previous drawers and an oversized wall cabinet, all filled with soaps and ointments, cosmetics, bandages, pills, and toothpastes are now reduced to fit into two small drawers and a mirrored hanging cabinet. I marvel at how well it works. There is no room for extras, but it works. The old bathroom rug reflects the blue in the new shower curtain, and best of all, the walk-in shower is a real treat.

Sheila's dried flowers hang in their small oval frame next to the mirror. The tiny Swiss wooden cow that Polly gave me stands incongruously on the windowsill next to the small aloe plant, an offshoot of the one that Johnathon left with me years ago. Is that what makes me feel at home, these mementos, gifts that bring me joy when they catch my eye?

I have not yet organized my books. Instead of being lined up in logical order next to their like-minded neighbors, they wait patiently, my dear old friends, sitting side by side with books of the same size and different topics. Books on aging mixed in with poetry and feminist theory; Jewish legends, travel tomes, and literary classics all on the same shelf; art books interspersed with oversized photo albums. I think it's good for them, this unaccustomed interdisciplinary proximity; let them learn and rub shoulders with each other. If only I could put my hands on the one I want when I want it. I spend precious time trying to find this or that volume when I need it. I cannot even be sure sometimes whether the book I'm looking for is hiding, or has found a new home through the library book sale before I moved.

This has been a major transition from living alone and eating alone, to a welcoming community of people my own age. Here at Kendal I can feel secure about the medical needs of my aging body, I can enjoy the social aspects of a vibrant group of peers. I like interacting with men again, meeting new friends and reconnecting with people who have been part of my life in Ithaca these many years and who knew Ben at Cornell.

Home is where the heart is, the saying goes. My heart and home will always hold cherished memories of loved ones, other homes, other objects, and other spaces, memories that nourish me. In this new home, I create new memories day by day.

My Bed

My bed is my refuge. When I was a little girl, staying in bed with some mild illness was delicious. I got Mutti's full attention, even concern, and comfort foods. I remember the soft cocoon of my goose-down quilt and the luxury of endless daydreams, half dozing in and out of real sleep. Then came a time when I started to explore the secret and forbidden passages of my young body, getting to know yet unnamed pleasurable sensations. Now staying in bed acquired the additional element of guilt and delight.

During the child-raising years of interrupted sleep, I could not get enough time in bed, with Ben or alone. In times of migraines and depression, I retreated to the darkness of my bedroom, shades drawn, safely bedded under the covers. In the days of premenstrual and menstrual cramps, I found bed a welcoming oasis in the fast pace of family life.

I shared my bed on frequent afternoons with one of my children, a deliciously sleeping toddler, at the stage when naptime was for me a welcome respite, and for the child an unwanted interruption of fun and games. Now, living alone, the only living being who shares my bed, and only at naptime, is my dog Boychick. Unlike the napping child of earlier days, he likes his nap as much as I do and curls up against my back, quite obviously content.

Fast forward now, past the years of marital bedtime games, enticements, avoidances, discoveries, adjustments, and the sheer ecstasy of shared intimacy. Past the years of serious illness, worried listening to Ben's breathing, and the annoyance of sexual deprivation and frustration.

My bed is still my refuge. Not only do I love stretching out between the cool sheets at night, I also flee to my bed when I am anxious or depressed, catching an extra nap here and there. At such times, sleep takes me for a time into a place free of conscious worry. As my body lets go of muscle tensions, the heavy feelings lose intensity. Unlike some folks who cannot sleep when they are upset, I can and do, and thereby find relief in bed. I love my bed, but sometimes with ambivalence.

After Ben died I avoided going to bed at night, staying up later and later. I hated being alone on my side, feeling the emptiness on his side. After a few months I gave away the king-size marital bed and bought a queen-size one, just for me. Bedtime avoidance gradually diminished and now I relish getting in between the sheets, my head on the Tempur-Pedic pillow that supports my aching neck. If only I didn't have to get up to pee during the night, but even then, it feels so good to get back into my very own and cozy nest.

Alarm clock buzzing
New day
Too soon

How They See Me at Kendal

She tries to walk straight, the old woman, but she weaves and wobbles a bit and has a slight limp, hardly noticeable, though she often uses a cane or a walker. She is plump and short, but not dowdy or bent over like some others. Her face is alert and often smiling, with a big hello for everyone, even when she does not remember your name. She knows who you are. She's with it, all right, but she just seems to blank out when it comes to names. She's pretty good at faking it, a broad smile in her voice instead of a name.

Sometimes she looks distracted and hurries along instead of stopping to chat as most of us do. She's on her way somewhere. She's a busy person, still involved in many things. She says the days go by too fast, she gets nothing done, but that's obviously not true. She's always off and running from one thing to another. Sometimes she's late coming into the dining room and looks around with a slightly forlorn glance to find a table that might welcome her, where folks are not yet finishing their dessert. She will often sit down with people she hardly knows and gets them talking about themselves.

We hear that she has traveled a lot, knows several languages. She takes off to see her family in Switzerland as if she were going to Trumansburg, or so it seems to us. Some of us really envy her. She says it's not for fun—that her brothers and sister are ailing. She does no tourist stuff when she's there, but still, we wish we could go.

She's a good writer, interviews newcomers for the Kendal *Breeze*. She is friendly but a little hard to get close to. Sometimes she seems aloof, sometimes a little pushy. But she can be helpful and listens to our concerns, our family stories, seems open to our confidences.

She is one of us.

Family Joys

I have come full circle now in my old age, deriving my greatest pleasure from my middle-aged sons and daughter and their offspring, the growing Siegel *mishpochah.*

My family has always been at the center of my emotional life. Now that I am no longer immersed in the career that has meant so much to me during the postparenting years, my family-related activities are again unrivaled in bringing joy to my soul. I see them at least once a year, some more often, and miss them between visits. Not living near each other, we keep in constant touch by phone, e-mail, Skype, and personal visits.

I find my biggest joy in witnessing my great-grandsons' wonder at discovering the world around them, no *naches* as emotionally satisfying as seeing my adult grandchildren coping successfully with work and family. When it comes to my two sons and daughter, nothing touches me more deeply than watching them develop into caring and responsible members of society and developing mature relationships with each other. Their joys are my joys and their hurdles and challenges are mine as well, but not mine to resolve. I am still learning that I cannot fix their problems, much as I would like to, and that I must respect their own efforts at coping with the inevitable life crises or disappointments that come their way. This is not easy for me.

Our family reunions of this past summer filled me with profound happiness. In June, we celebrated Tommy and Sarah's wedding in a beautiful botanical garden in Maine, with their young sons, Rylan and Maxwell, under the chuppah. In August it was Sarah and Alan's turn on the grounds of the impressive Vancouver Museum of Anthropology.

Our family keeps expanding, more loves, more warmth, more lives to care about. Not to ignore the many challenges, illnesses, pains, and losses that are inevitable in every family. The unexpected death of Johnathon at age twenty-five still haunts us all; we have mourned together. We have muddled through the times of stress and distancing, and moved beyond our disagreements. We are not an ideal family, but we have never stopped loving each other.

So I count my blessings. My four siblings are still alive. Rose, now ninety-five, needs full-time care. She lives in Lausanne with Sam, who just turned ninety. David has Alzheimer's. He is ninety-two, lives with his dear wife, Tanya, in Geneva. Fenny, age eighty-three, lives with her husband, Benjamin, in Kfar Shmaryahu, Israel. I try to visit once a year. We live apart and each live our lives very differently, yet our bonds are close and we marvel at our longevity.

I have also been blessed with friendships that continue to enrich my life. Many of my dearest friends have died and left me with a legacy of colorful memories. The few who are still with me share the small pleasures of daily life, a casual meal, an occasional concert or a play. And most important, we have great conversations, exchange ideas, talk politics, and reminiscences. My new companions at Kendal also help to keep life interesting and loneliness at bay.

My life is punctuated with moments and days of deep contentment when I am among my growing brood. I marvel at my good fortune, at the love that flows among us. Words cannot convey the joy of watching my children mature into midlife, my grandchildren take on adult relationships and responsibilities, and their little ones develop full of promise.

January 1, 2010

January 1, 2010, the first day of the new year, the first day of the new decade. Alone at midnight at my kitchen table, playing solitaire, just watching the clock to welcome in the annual beginning. This symbolic moment of change feels like any other midnight, but should perhaps feel momentous.

Strange to celebrate a first at age eighty-five. It might be more appropriate to celebrate the years gone by, the many firsts, the many beginnings. Will I see another new decade? Will I be alive and well in 2020? Let me not go there, though I do. Let me take it one year at a time. I can contemplate the year ahead with some confidence. I have plans, a month in California, Pesach at home with family, another trip to Europe, hopefully not to a funeral.

Is it confidence or realistic hope that sustains me? Reality has two sides or more. Reality tells me that I am in good health and spirits, that I will make it through the coming year and more. Reality also tells me that the certainty of death gets closer every year; accidents or illness may occur. Reality tells me that my siblings and I are living on borrowed time, one of us is sure to go sooner or later. We have lived a good long life, outlived many loved ones. Who will be first among the five of us?

I watch the snow fall gently over the winter landscape, becoming a white screen, like a cocoon, a nest, keeping me safe in the comfort of my home. I need not go out. Modern technology, literally at my fingertips, keeps me from feeling isolated. The phone rings, friends call, e-mails arrive, family members check in. We exchange good wishes, heart to heart over unseen waves.

I feel the wonder of it all, the wonder of the natural world in winter glory, the wonder of human accomplishments that ease, amuse, enhance my daily life. I feel the wonder of being safe, well fed, alive and well in 2010, when others are caught in the ravages of weather, war, and hunger.

Words cannot tell how deep my gratitude, but acts of charity may ease my troubled soul. I date the first check with unfamiliar numbers. The first day of the New Year has begun.

The Cabbage Mystery, September 2010

Flat on my back in the tiny hospital room, I heard them talking in the hall. The door was ajar. The doctors were making their morning rounds, their voices dimly penetrating my drowsy state. I thought I must have misheard what they were saying.

I had left my hearing aids at home, afraid they might get lost in my move from the preop floor to the operating theater, to the ICU, and later to the cardiac postop unit on the fourth floor.

I heard them again talking about cabbages. "Cabbage two days," I heard, and a bit later, "Triple cabbage twenty-four hours." What on earth could this mean? By the time they had reached my room, I was anxious and eager to hear about my own progress, never mind asking about cabbages.

On my fifth day, having repeatedly overheard talk of cabbages, I finally got around to asking one of the nurses what cabbages were doing on the cardiac unit.

"Oh that," the nurse replied. "That's what you've had. You've had a double cabbage."

"I have?" I asked dubiously.

"Sure, CABG, cardiac artery bypass graft, that's what you've had." I giggled quietly; a hearty laugh would have been too painful so soon after my cabbage.

December 31, 2010

Thank the goddess this year is over.

I could have done without this past year's pain, anxiety, surgeries, hospitalizations, limitations, and recuperations that made me finally so very grateful to be alive and well.

No, this has not been a normal year. And yet, and yet, the good stuff has been spectacular and comes close to outweighing the bad stuff.

I found out that my body was strong enough to recover from a hip replacement on June 15, our wedding anniversary, an angiogram on August 13, my birthday, and a double cardiac bypass on September 8, Erev Rosh HaShanah. All this went smoothly, without side effects. No stroke, no death, no memory loss, no major depression. I have developed a new sense of my own resilience, balanced by a new sense of my proximity to death. I feel more vulnerable, more prone to body malfunctions, more likely to need medical or surgical interventions. I also feel unsteady on my feet, at risk of falling, yet determined to keep living as fully as I'm able. My days are filled with medical appointments, cardiac rehab activities, and water aerobics.

The good stuff is still with me. I always knew that my sons and daughter love me, that they are deeply caring individuals, and that I could count on their help when needed. Knowing theoretically and seeing them in action are two different kinds of knowing. The generous care that Charlie, Barry, and Ruth lavished upon me during these medical crises has filled me with a deep sense of their love and made me immensely grateful for who they are. They took turns being with me during surgeries, during medical consultations, and during transitions from hospital to assisted living, and back to home, not once, but several times. Competent, thoughtful, and generous, they have made me feel secure not only in their future care of me, but in the values and priorities of their own lives. Sarah and Alan's stint of helpfulness touched me deeply, and Sam's presence during the heart surgery meant more than I can say.

May they and all our loved ones continue to live fully and be well.

LIFE JOURNEYS AND PERSONAL DEVELOPMENT

These autobiographical essays have been adapted
from previously published papers

Childhood Migrations[1]

My childhood was like a hidden storm under calm waters, or was it a calm sea under stormy clouds? I was somehow aware of the ripples of danger, the undercurrents of adult fears, unspoken messages, half-hidden from childish ears.

I was born in Berlin, Germany, on August 13, 1924. My parents, Pinkus Zachar Zelig Josefowitz and Frieda Shur Josefowitz, had recently migrated from Anikst, their small Lithuanian hometown in the province of Kovno. My older sister Rose (1916) and brother David (1918) had been born in Kharkov, Russia; brother Samuel (1921) in Anikst after the family had returned to Lithuania because of the Russian Revolution. A period of famine in Lithuania caused many Lithuanian

---

[1] Adapted from Biographical Statement included in archives submitted to Schlesinger Library at Radcliffe.

Jews, including my family, to move to Germany in the early 1920s.

My earliest years were spent in a stately home in Berlin, at Preussen Allee 15, cared for by Anni, our German nanny and governess. I attended first grade at the public school down the block. I remember Anni as strict and punitive, my parents as warm and loving. Papa was often absent on business trips for long periods. I heard my parents speak Russian and Yiddish to each other, but my first language was German, spoken at home and in school. My younger sister Fenny was born in 1929 when I was five.

In 1930 our family gave up the house in Berlin and moved to Lausanne, Switzerland. My older siblings had been exposed to earlier and more traumatic upheavals and changes of language. I learned much later, as an adult, that although Hitler was not yet in power, anti-Semitism in Germany had become much more overt, prompting my father to move our family at that time. He said that he had learned his lesson during the Russian Revolution and would not wait until it was too late to flee.

After a few weeks of hotel living, we moved into a huge mansion on the hill, called the Château du Signal. Anni soon returned to Germany and was replaced by a series of governesses whose primary job was to take care of the infant Fenny. The nearest school, almost across the street, was a girl's boarding school where I was the only *externe,* commuter, and younger than the other girls, who were mostly British. The intent was for me to learn French.

In that unaccustomed setting, replete with not one, but two new languages, I was a lost soul. One day, leaving home with much reluctance, I arrived at the usual side door that would be opened in response to my ring, and the response was slow. I turned around and ran back home, telling my mother that they had not let me in. I remember this incident as the only time that I acted out my unhappiness, and felt oh so guilty. But the comfort of my mother's arms, of being home even for a short respite, was worth the lie and the guilt. Nothing changed. I was mildly scolded but not punished and sent back to school after inquiries had been made. I began to learn French in this strange environment, and a few words of English from the other girls who never befriended me, the outsider.

The following year I was placed at l'École Nouvelle, a boys' school that my brothers attended, where a few grades of elementary school were coeducational. We soon moved from the château into a large first-floor apartment at 7 Chemin du Levant, nearer town and I was able to walk to school with my brothers.

I think it was fourth grade when I was accepted at l'École Supérieure de Jeunes Filles, the public school for girls who were university bound. The school was downtown and I became quite independent, walked downhill to school twice a day, home for lunch, and trekked back uphill or took the tramway home in the afternoon. I continued piano lessons, which had started at age five in Berlin, but now I walked to my teacher's home, rather than having the teacher come to our house. I joined the *éclaireuses*, Girl Scouts, and went on school hikes in the Swiss countryside and nearby mountains. It was a healthy childhood, lots of fresh air, hiking, biking, swimming, and skiing in Arosa on our yearly winter vacations. Several summers were spent at the beach in Deauville and Trouville, France, where my parents rented a villa. Later I remember some summers at mountain resorts. I still remember our Lausanne phone number, 31 9 39, in French, and I generally continue to count in French.

I don't know why we moved to Zürich when I was eleven. It must have been 1935. My memories of Zürich are not as clear or as fond as those of Lausanne. I never felt as much at home speaking Schwyzerdütsch, the Swiss

German dialect that I now spoke with schoolmates, while instruction was mostly in German. I was not accustomed to male teachers who were not as gentle as my previous female teachers had been. The language and the curriculum were different, yet I was expected to adjust without causing any problems. I did not pass the oral exam that separated the university-bound students from the rest, and so spent two years in a class of kids with lower expectations. Again the outsider, I developed headaches and was probably depressed.

Always the outsider, always adjusting to new cultures as if there was nothing to it. Our parents expected us to do well, no matter what. My troubles were not considered troubles within the larger context of fleeing from overt anti-Semitism and imminent war. I never questioned the changing of schools, migrations from country to country, new languages to learn, from German to French, to Schwyzerdütsch, and later to English, while parents and other relatives spoke Russian and Yiddish to each other. I did not know that this was unusual, assumed that it was no big deal, perfectly normal. I tried hard to go with the flow, not to add to the larger worries of my parents.

By now, we were aware of the hostile treatment of Jews in Germany and were not comfortable speaking erman in public. Tensions increased, as Jewish refugees began fleeing through Switzerland, sometimes being sheltered in our home for a few nights. In 1938, my paternal grandparents fled Vienna soon after Hitler had invaded Austria, having experienced a frightening visit from the Gestapo. They moved into rented rooms near us.

My parents were proudly Jewish, but not very observant. They joined and supported the local synagogue, which we attended only on the High Holidays. It was and still is a beautiful building. My father and brothers sat downstairs, where I could look down at them from the women's balcony. My brothers were privately and minimally prepared for their Bar Mitzvahs, but my sisters and I had no Jewish education. My mother kept a kosher household and did much of the cooking herself, though we always had a cook and other servants. The family socialized only with other Jewish families, but I had many friends among non-Jews. I was usually the only Jewish child in my class.

Most of the time, I felt comfort and security within our close-knit family. Papa was often absent on business trips. Mutti was always home, busy and reassuringly competent. My two older brothers teased me but also protected me. My older sister tried to teach me the ways of the new culture faster than my mother could, and I resented it, perceived it as bullying. My younger sister hated each new nanny and I tried to comfort her. All said, however, my overwhelming feeling was one of belonging in this noisy, articulate household, where Mutti was always there, good meals were served on time, birthdays were celebrated, jokes and pranks abounded, and we liked each other, bonded against the outside world.

When I remember my childhood, mostly in Switzerland, the images that emerge are of boisterous, happy times around the dining table, Papa's laughter and his loud scoldings, long, solitary walks to school in Zürich and Lausanne, and generally good times in school, in spite of painful episodes during transitions. And they were painful, these early mistakes, misunderstandings, ignorance of new customs, using the wrong phrase at the wrong time, and always being the outsider. I remember wanting so much to belong, to be a Swiss child, singing patriotic songs with gusto as if they were mine. And I remember the deep letdown when I occasionally was reminded at home to be on my guard, because "they" could turn against us at any time; "they" could turn us out, revoke our resident permits, and where would we be then, where would we go?

Our Jewish family no longer felt safe in Europe, fearing that Hitler might invade Switzerland. In 1938 the family was suddenly spread apart. My brothers were sent to the United States. David, having completed a year at the Eidgenössische Technische Hochschule in Zürich, was admitted to MIT; Sam went to RPI, Rensselaer Polytechnic Institute. Rose was studying at the Sorbonne in Paris, and Fenny was placed in a Swiss boarding school. I was the only child still at home when we moved back from Zürich to Lausanne. We had barely occupied our new apartment when my father was diagnosed with severe stomach ulcers and went to a private clinic with my mother. I was fourteen at that time, alone in our new home with a newly hired and inexperienced housekeeper. Accustomed as I had been to a noisy household of parents, four siblings, and familiar household helpers, I felt acutely alone. Back again at l'École Supérieure, I had a lot of catching up to do, including first-year English and Latin.

In the spring of 1939, trunks were packed, furniture shipped in a 'lift', and my parents, sisters, and I set sail for New York, first class on the Queen Mary. My mother and I were seasick all the way.

Having entered the United States on a visitor's visa, we soon traveled to Montreal, where we spent the next nine months until we were able to reenter the United States with more permanent papers. Memories of private school in Montreal are a blur, trying to read *Macbeth* with a minimal command of English and no background in British history. We finally settled into a New York apartment at 285 Central Park West, which still belongs to the family.

Rachel & Ben
Simmons Junior Prom, 1943

From Immigrant to US Citizen[2]

I arrived at Simmons almost by accident. I was barely sixteen, a new European immigrant who had passed the College Board exams with near-perfect scores in French, German, English, and European History. My education in Swiss schools had been rigorous, but erratic and incomplete.

---

2   Adapted from "From Immigrant to Citizen," *Simmons Review* (Winter 1995).

As Lithuanian Jews, my parents had feared the long arm of Hitler's European invasions, and his persecution of all Jews. They decided to leave our temporary home in Switzerland for the hope of a more secure future in America. We sailed for the United States in the spring of 1939, a few months before the war began. My aunt Minnie and uncle Hy in Newton, Massachusetts, convinced us that I should study in Boston, the home of all the best colleges and universities.

I walked into the Simmons College admissions office by myself in mid-August of 1940, and I still don't know on what grounds I convinced the admissions officer to admit me to the waiting list. Perhaps it was my apparent poise and independence, perhaps it was that Radcliffe had also admitted me to their waiting list, or that I spoke nearly flawless English, or that I was taking a course at Harvard Summer School. Perhaps it was simply that Simmons needed one more dormitory student able to pay full tuition. I was notified three days before the term began that I was admitted to the freshman class.

Admitted, but totally unprepared. Neither my parents nor I had any idea what the academic or social life on an American college campus was like. Furthermore, my parents were much too involved in their own resettlement and insecurities to be of much support to me. It was Rose, my older sister, who took me shopping and brought me to the dorm from New York, where the family was still living in a hotel. My brother, who was at MIT, had his own, not always accurate, version of the mysteries of late adolescence in America; dating, and football games, and all those terribly important but unfamiliar customs of a new country. My classmates, who were experiencing their own transition, at least shared a common language and history with each other, as well as the background of an American high school. I did not.

Was I the only Jewish girl in my freshman dorm? I know that I was the only immigrant. To say that I felt confused and forlorn is a gross understatement. That first year, I could barely keep up with the readings in my classes. My study skills were geared to the tightly structured methods of a Swiss classroom, and my command of English, though superficially impressive, was actually very limited. I flunked American History, struggling through the textbook without understanding many key words and concepts, having never been exposed to the subject before. I'm not sure just how I managed to pass my other courses. At the end of the year I was put on probation and called in to the dean's office.

I entered with fear and trepidation, expecting a harsh scolding. Dean Mesick gave me a lesson in positive reinforcement and in social skills that I have valued for the rest of my life. Somehow, she let me know that this interview was intended to help me rather than to embarrass me or to find fault. She was the first and only person to ask me what the problem was, and she gave me my first opportunity to name the difficulties of studying a foreign culture in a foreign language. When she inquired about my friendships and social life in the dorm, I confided that I had not really made any friends, and that the other girls (we did not refer to ourselves as women) seemed to ignore me. Had it occurred to me, she asked, that the other girls might be just as shy as I was, just as fearful of rejection, and might even be intimidated by my otherness? She informed me that I was as capable as the next one to take the lead in approaching another person, and that I could begin to take some responsibility for making friends, even when I felt shy about doing so. I heard her, and she made a difference. I felt empowered, though neither Dean Mesick nor I would have used that language at the time.

From then on, my Simmons experience became more positive. I took more initiative in reaching out to other girls. During my junior and senior years on the fifth floor at Evans Hall, I formed two lifelong friendships with my classmates Marion Secunda Poliakoff and Beverly Kerness Unger, and I became friends with Louise Chen, who was, as far as I can tell, the only other foreign student at Simmons during those years.

I gave up my dream of becoming a medically trained psychoanalyst, choosing instead to work toward a degree in psychology or social work. I changed my major from a premed science concentration to what was then called a preprofessional program, focusing on the social sciences. I remember best my courses in sociology, psychology, economics, labor relations, the family, and an introductory social work course.

As graduation day approached, I did not feel ready to go on with career preparations. I had fallen in love with Benjamin Morton Siegel and got married to him three days after graduation. Soon, like many of my classmates, I became a full-time mother, homemaker, and community volunteer.

Though it took me another twenty-five years before I returned to graduate school, I was still interested in becoming a therapist. During those child-raising years, I had continued to read in the social sciences and had developed some significant group work and organizational skills in my volunteer work. I began to realize that my Simmons studies had provided a solid grounding for all these activities and for my new latelife career as a socialworker, feminist therapist, and writer.

More significant, perhaps, is the fact that my social science courses at Simmons also gave me an education in American citizenship and an exposure to American norms and ideals that were an important part of my Americanization process. It was at Simmons that I acquired the knowledge base that has fueled my ongoing participation in the life of my community, as a professional and a volunteer, as a voter and a community activist.

My Names and My Jewish Identity[3]

The biblical name Rachel has varied spellings and pronunciations. These variations have followed me through our early migrations and later travels, conveying what it is like to be a wandering Jew. The story of my names can tell you who I am and how I grew into the feminist *alte Yiddene* (old Jewish woman) of today. It is a story of Jewish migrations, of a close family clan scattered over four continents, of a family's richly varied approaches to being Jewish, and of the Jewish choices I have made during eighty-seven years of defining and redefining my Jewish identity.

---

[3] Adapted from "My Names," in *A Minyan of Women: Family Dynamics, Jewish Identity and Psychotherapy Practice,* guest eds. Beverly Greene and Dorith Brodbar (Philadelphia, PA: Taylor & Francis, 2010).

My mother was still grieving her own mother's untimely death when I was born. The night before she was to have aborted me, she dreamt that I would be a girl who would carry her departed mother's name. She called off the abortion and named me *Rochel Gitel*, my Yiddish name. Grandmother Rochel Gitel's large sepia photograph hung in my parents' bedroom in an oval frame, next to and matching the one of grandfather Rav Eliahu Dov Shur. Her beautiful face conveyed to me a sense of inner peace and goodness that engraved itself into my Jewish consciousness. Did I not owe my life to her? Was I not destined to become the carrier of Jewish tradition and values in my family?

At home I was called Rochale, the Yiddish name of *shtetl* ancestry. In Berlin, my first-grade teacher called me by the German version, Rahel. In Lausanne, I grew to love the French appellation of Rachel, pronounced Rashelle; it is still my favorite way of being called. Arriving in New York at age fourteen, the English version, pronounced Raichel, sounded strange and harsh to me; I did not want to give up the softer and familiar sound of Rashelle. At Simmons, looking for a nickname, they started calling me Rocky; I was relieved when that name did not stick. Back to Rashelle, or as close as Americans can wrap their tongues around it; it often sounds more like Roshelle. I can live with that. Because I continue to spell my name "Rachel" it is often pronounced in English and I have ceased to care about that. During our year in Jerusalem, Israelis pronounced Rachel in Hebrew, with the guttural *ch*; it felt appropriate and truly Jewish.

Like a chameleon, responding to any given linguistic environment, I continue to answer to each of these pronunciations, but for a long time I wondered which was my one, true name. I have since come to feel at peace with the knowledge that all the ways of saying and spelling my name are truly who I am, the wandering Jewish woman with a biblical name, pronounced in many languages, at home in many places.

My parents spoke German among Germans and Yiddish or Russian to each other and at times to us. My father's loud quarrels with his brothers were always in Russian. Our nanny spoke German, which I consider my first language. Within the family, we called each other by our Yiddish diminutives: sister Rose was *Raisale*, brother David was *Dodik* or *Dodale*, brother Samuel answered to *Shmulik* or *Mulik*. When sister Fenny was born, we called her *Feigale*. We called our parents *Papa* and *Mutti*, the German words for dad and mom. In later years when they became sick or elderly we called them *Papale* and *Mammale*, in Yiddish.

We were not a religiously observant family. My mother kept a kosher kitchen as long as her father was alive, in case he ever came to visit. We went to services on the High Holidays, father in his top hat and all of us in new garments, and we always celebrated a festive family Seder. Jewishness pervaded our home in tense and worried conversations about the fate of other Jews, in social interactions with Jews, and in acts of rescue and caring for Jews less fortunate than ourselves. We felt a heightened sense of alertness or even preparedness for potential anti-Semitism, verging at times on paranoia. We learned and tried to conform to the social norms of our host country as best we knew how. Unlike many Western European Jews of that period, however, our family took pride in identifying ourselves as Jews. Furthermore, my parents claimed a distinguished Jewish ancestry, based on generations of rabbis on my mother's side, and successful merchants on the side of my father. They relished telling us that both sets of parents had disapproved of their marriage because Papa was not *frum* (religiously observant) enough for Rabbi Shur's blessing, and Mutti was not rich enough to please grandfather Josefowitz.

I was told that I had a *yiddishe neshoma*, a Jewish soul; I wondered what that meant but was happy to claim it. In school I was nearly always the only Jew in my class. I had non-Jewish friends, and I joined the Girl Scouts, but our family never interacted with their families. I yearned to be Swiss as well as Jewish, but I knew that we were aliens, not even immigrants, depending on temporary residence permits. Tales of German atrocities drifted into our temporary haven, and Jewish refugees frequently sought shelter in our home. As the feeling of impending war escalated, my family began to plan our own exodus to America. We arrived in New York in March of 1939.

Fast forward. One of the things that attracted me to Ben, the American-born Jewish man that I married at age nineteen, was that with him I would somehow "belong," both as a Jew and as an American. No more wandering, no more feeling like an alien, an immigrant. With him I could live my version of the American dream, become a Jewish American wife and mother, a member of the Jewish community, conveying Jewish values and American norms to our future children. I joined him in his strong Zionism and active Jewish observance, though I bristled at his imposition of certain restrictions on my customary Saturday activities. We muddled through these early signs of disagreement, not letting them interfere with the strength of our love and desire for each other.

In the home that we created together for our children we embraced traditional Jewish customs. I kept a kosher kitchen. We enjoyed Friday night and Holiday home celebrations. I studied Hebrew, and we joined the Conservative Temple in Ithaca, New York, as soon as we arrived in what was to be our permanent home. I became active in the local Hadassah chapter. Our closest friends were more observant than we had been and far better educated in Judaism. I tried hard to catch up and fit in, but I also joined and took on leadership roles in the non-Jewish world of community organizations like the PTA, Cornell Campus Club, and Engineering Women's Club.

My life as a Jewish mother, faculty wife, and community volunteer was rich in rewards, personal connections, Jewish traditions, and intellectual stimulation. So why the migraines, the bouts of depression? Looking back, I know now that no one, including myself, had ever acknowledged the trauma of my early uprootings, of not knowing which of my names was my real name.

When did I change? When did I realize that our marriage could tolerate open disagreement instead of subversive resistance, and that I could develop my own ideas, my own preferences? Change and awareness came gradually, after Ben's first heart attack in 1961 and after the children left home. Change and awareness came again in the early 1970s while I was back in graduate school, when my now-adult daughter shocked me into feminist awareness, and definitely when the women's movement became part of my consciousness. When I began my professional career and started to write, I found that I could trust my own ideas and speak them loud and clear.

I began to read the works of women, to attend conferences, to meet and talk with other emerging feminists. Within this early feminist sisterhood, I found the courage to look inward and seek an understanding of my own experience of otherness. It was an exciting, tumultuous time. Being Jewish and female was at the center of my feminist awakening. My first published article was entitled, "The Jew as a Woman" in *The Jewish Spectator.*

My husband, Ben, was a man of letters; he believed in the written word. At first, he was unable to hear me when I ranted and raved about my discontent with Jewish discrimination against women. It was only when my words were written and published that he began to understand what I had been saying. He became my ally, presenting the case for women's inclusion in the Torah service to our temple board, at a time when there were no women on that board.

While becoming a therapist, working with women who were less privileged and more oppressed than I, I gradually acquired the feminist lens that I could now focus on the condition of Jewish women. I became more openly vocal as a Jew, a feminist, and a writer. I questioned male centeredness and male authorities not only on matters of psychotherapy but also more specifically on Jewish issues. I advocated for the inclusion of women in all aspects of Jewish ritual at home and in the synagogue.

In my fifties, in the process of writing, my public voice became stronger, eventually more nuanced. It is a Jewish voice. It is the voice of a feminist therapist, an aging mother/grandmother/great-grandmother, a widow, now a retiree, and always a Jewish woman. It is in that voice that I coedited the three collections of Jewish women's essays in collaboration with my good friend Ellen Cole (1991, 1997, 2000) and my niece Susan Steinberg Oren (2000). The work of selecting and editing these personal articles was a wondrous experience. I felt, at times, that I was at the heart of a widely scattered Jewish women's community, and I relished the fullness and flavor of our connections to each other, the intimacy of sharing the Jewish aspects of our lives.

At home, and at my insistence, Ben began taking over some of the Passover preparations that I had found so burdensome. We feminized our reading of the Passover Haggadah, turned the story of the four sons into one about four children, and inserted the midwives into the reading of the Haggadah. I fought for changes in prayer language and synagogue observance in my own congregation. These innovations were much disputed at the time; they have now became a normal part of Conservative, Reconstructionist, and Reform Jewish ritual and are taken for granted in many Jewish homes.

The first time that I was called to the Torah to recite the blessings preceding the Torah reading, I felt as if I was breaking an ancient taboo. Would the heavens open up to swallow me and my congregation? Or worse yet, would I commit the sin of misreading the holy words or the Hebrew chant and embarrass myself as well? I stood there, hiding my emotion, proud and tall, and trembling inside with a mixture of fear and excitement.

A strange thing happened to me after some years of Jewish advocacy. Having fought so hard to have women included in previously male enclaves of Jewish life, I began to have doubts about perpetuating those very same Jewish customs and traditions. I found so much that was contrary to my own humanitarian and feminist values. Now that we got in, is that where we wanted to be? Unlike many of my sister Jewish feminists who took every opportunity to quench their thirst for Jewish learning by studying Torah, I have resisted such immersion, knowing that my anger would get in the way of genuine learning. I have only occasionally approached the study of ancient text and liturgy, finding many questions and few answers.

While my Jewish activism has been directed at the synagogue, and I feel a strong sense of community within my congregation, my Jewish identity and activities have not been primarily focused on organized religion or regular synagogue services. Now that women are full participants, I enjoy the familiar chants, the pomp and circumstance of the Torah service, but I find no personal meaning in the actual prayer language.

Nevertheless, on the High Holidays, I celebrate Rosh HaShanah, the Jewish New Year, and Yom Kippur, the Day of Atonement, in the sanctuary of my Temple Beth El congregation. There, in this familiar setting, replete with meaningful memories, I find deep spiritual meaning and a sense of connection with Klal Israel (the Jewish people).

Family Seders have had an evolution of their own in response to the ages of children, grandchildren, and now great-grandchildren. After Ben's death in 1990, I began to lead the Seder myself and to co-lead it with my grown sons and daughter (Siegel 1997). Having established my right and my ability to do so, I am now content to sit back and enjoy the Seders led by Charles, Hyam, and Ruth. On Friday nights, I often share the meal with my friends Barbara Johnson and Nicky Morris, both Jews by choice, whose wholehearted, enthusiastic singing fills my heart with *shabbos* spirit.

My Jewish allegiances, interests, and activities reach far and wide, beyond my family, my congregation, and my feminist sisterhood, and into the language and culture of my parents, the horrors of the Holocaust, and the complexities of Jewish life in Israel.

My connection to Israel, my love of the land, the history, and the people, became intense during the year we spent in Jerusalem in 1961. So much has changed since then. Israel is no longer the idealistic land of early settlers and of *kibbutzim*, primarily a refuge of Holocaust survivors. My unease with Israeli politics and government policies began during the war with

Lebanon and has grown ever since. I weep at every suicide bombing and I weep at every Israeli retaliation. I fear for the safety of my sister Fenny and her children and grandchildren. I despair at the generations of young people on both sides learning hatred and cruelty. And I feel frustrated by my own powerlessness.

After some fifty years of avoiding films and literature about the Holocaust, my work with Holocaust survivors and their children has led me to an immersion in Holocaust literature. I began to read women's memoirs of that period and have learned to tolerate more of the agony. In 1997, during a trip to Eastern Europe, I stood at the mass grave in the Warsaw Jewish cemetery, unable to cry. I returned from Theresienstadt unable to speak of what I had seen and felt. On Rosh HaShanah of that year, I said *kaddish* for the six million Jews, the Gypsies, the gays, and the others who had been so savagely murdered.

My Jewish life has become more secular as I get older. Now in late life, I feel a strong pull to reconnect with my Jewish roots and to convey some of my cultural and linguistic Jewish inheritance to my middle-aged children and grandchildren. I have, for example, traveled to Switzerland and Berlin with Sarah and Brenda, two of my granddaughters, showing them the streets where I grew up. I have gathered a genealogy of my extended family, bridging seven generations, from my great-grandparents to great-grandchildren, and tracing my extended family, the *mishpochah* that is scattered in Europe, Israel, North America, Australia, and South Africa. I also enjoy every opportunity to speak Yiddish, joined a Yiddish-speaking group, and discovered that I have retained much more of the overheard language than I was aware of.

Now that I live alone and have been widowed more than twenty years, I continue to make subtle changes in my expressions of Jewish identity. I feel less bound by the earlier influences of family, spouse, and social environment. The components of my Jewish identity keep changing and growing. I continue to find more sources of pleasure, more puzzles, more arguments in my engagement with being a Jewish woman.

I've come a long way in my Jewish journey and it is not over. I have found, within feminism and feminist therapy, the tools and training to fully appreciate my Jewish history and identity. I relish my own kaleidoscope of Jewish memories and images. My heritage of acute Jewish pain has been tempered by the cultural, humorous, and spiritual richness of that same heritage.

I have been conscious of being Jewish all my life and have consciously and deliberately questioned my Jewish decisions, yet many of my Jewish experiences, activities and attitudes come from a place of habit, familiarity, nostalgia, and even sentimentality, which defy conscious analysis.

My names embody the paths and detours of my Jewish wanderings, the connections and disconnections with Jewish and non-Jewish cultures, the complex relationships with Jewish and non-Jewish friends, colleagues, and family members. Each of my names carries colorful associations and memories. I no longer worry about who I am or which of my names is my true name, for they all are.

I hope that the Jewish flavor of my long life has been conveyed in the vignettes and memories that I have written in my weekly writing circle and included in this book.

Beyond the Role of Wife and Mother[4]

Exploring New Possibilities

In 1960-61 we spent Ben's sabbatical in Jerusalem. I attended an *ulpan* (Hebrew language immersion program) where I achieved a minimal proficiency in speaking Hebrew; my reading and writing skills are still halting at best. The year in Israel was full of wonders, exposure to new friends, new ideas and experiences, as well as significant tensions. Ben and I came to Israel with a deep commitment to the Zionist ideal. We loved the land and its biblical associations, and we felt the emotional pull to make *alyah* (Israeli immigration).

---

[4]   Adapted from Biographical Statement included in archives submitted to Schlesinger Library at Radcliffe.

While there, we realized that we were not suited for the then still-harsh realities of Israeli life, including military service for our children. We both agonized about this decision and painfully experienced the loss of a dream. Ben suffered a serious heart attack in London on our way home.

This traumatic event, combined with the stressful soul-searching of our Israeli stay, and our firstborn son's leaving home for college, launched me into a profound reassessment of my life patterns and life goals. During Ben's slow recovery, I searched for new meaning in my life, beyond the role of wife and mother. For the first time in my life, I saw myself as a separate person, no longer blindly and automatically relying on my husband's guidance. I had suddenly grown up at age thirty-eight. I did not at that time know how to put these feelings into words. I did, however, know that I had to actively engage in some new activities outside the home.

My faculty wife status gave me easy access to classes at Cornell where I could explore new directions. I first enrolled in a poetry course. Looking back, I would say that this was my first attempt to write in a structured and meaningful fashion. Later that summer, I took a typing course where I earned the lowest grade in the class but was also graded as the most improved. Then followed some summer courses relating to the teaching of underachievers, which I found helpful in my volunteer positions, tutoring kids in the local school system and organizing a program of junior high students tutoring their peers. I also found the intellectual stimulation invigorating. After a year of being a teacher aide in a class for emotionally disturbed elementary school children, I volunteered to be the acting director of the Hebrew School at Temple Beth El while the congregation was looking for a new rabbi/school director.

During my volunteer years after Ben's heart attack, life at home was far from peaceful and was filled with major transitions in our family. Ben's recovery was slow and his health precarious. Our entry into the post-parenting years was tumultuous. The Vietnam War and the drug culture had a deeply unsettling effect on our teenage children. Charles and Barry were able to escape the draft for medical reasons, but not without much agonizing. Ruth graduated high school in 1968 and left home to attend the Hebrew University in Jerusalem. Hyam Barry got married in 1970 without finishing college. Johnathon, our first grandchild, was born the following year while we were on sabbatical leave in La Jolla, California. Charles was by now in graduate school at Yale.

In 1969, I had a hysterectomy to remove a benign tumor. This real and symbolic ending of my reproductive years left me feeling useless, depressed, and grieving my primary role. I had internalized the powerful messages about mothering as a woman's sole function in life. My journey toward a career outside the home, begun after Ben's heart attack, now took on a new immediacy.

At Cornell, the graduate advisor in the School of Human Ecology told me that Cornell was not interested in letting me enter a graduate program unless my goal was to do research or to teach at the university level. I began to look elsewhere into graduate programs in social work. During our sabbatical semester in La Jolla, in 1971, I took two extension courses at the University of California in San Diego. The first was an experiential course in group therapy; the second, a course on the interactions of stress and illness. I also participated in some social work volunteer activities at the San Diego Jewish Family Service agency. I applied to the Syracuse School of Social Work and was accepted for the following fall.

I discovered that my brain was still functioning and that I was already familiar with much current mental health literature. I also discovered that I knew nothing about the lives of people less privileged than I had always been. In my fieldwork, I interned first at the Family and Children's Services agency in Ithaca and then at the Tompkins County Mental Health Clinic. There, upon earning my MSW, I was hired as staff social worker. I became painfully aware of the physical and emotional abuse of women. The women's movement began to make sense to me. I also began to recognize the privileges of my own life, which I had always taken for granted

While in graduate school, commuting to Syracuse, I began psychoanalysis with Dr. Robert Seidenberg. In his office, I gained the courage to clarify my own thoughts, to put them into words, and to speak up in my own voice.

Becoming a Feminist Psychotherapist

During that time, I began to attend some professional conferences that focused on women's issues. There, in the presence of feminist colleagues, I was encouraged to practice and improve my newfound skills of public speaking, writing, editing, and organizing. I read the emerging women's literature voraciously. My first conference was a pre-conference Women's Institute at the 1976 American Orthopsychiatry Association annual meeting in San Francisco, led and organized by Dr. Jean Baker Miller. The following year I attended the Ortho Institute in Baltimore. I presented my first paper in 1978 in Toronto. When I proposed that we assemble some of the Ortho Women's Institute papers into a publication, Joan Hammerman Robbins volunteered to coedit the book with me. Together, we began the work on what became *Women Changing Therapy.* When I came home from Toronto and recounted these developments to my friend Hanna Aber, her reply was "*Ganz wie die Grossen,*" a German expression meaning "As if you were a grown-up." Alexandra Kaplan and I became co-organizers of the next year's Institute, which was held in New York City.

I believe it was 1979 when I attended my first Association for Women in Psychology meeting in Boston. There I met with a small ad hoc gathering of women interested in feminist psychotherapy on an "advanced" level. I remember the presence of Lenore Walker, Adrienne Smith, Ruth Siegel (not my daughter), and possibly Barbara Claster. We talked about inviting other feminist therapists to a gathering the following year; Lenore volunteered to organize it. The Feminist Therapy Institute was conceived in that room. That winter we all saw each other again at the

First International Interdisciplinary Women's Studies Conference in Haifa, Israel. In March 1980, fifty women who were to become the nucleus of the Feminist Therapy Institute met in Vail, Colorado, where we each presented a ten-minute work in progress. The following year we drafted our bylaws during our conference in Washington, DC,

These were heady years; excitement and creativity ran high. It was sisterhood at its best, a honeymoon period among feminists. At that time, our need to connect with each other was stronger than any need to differentiate among us. We challenged existing theories, assumptions, and mental health practices. We began to listen more vigorously to our own experiences and those of our clients, rather than relying on established and male-centered experts in the field.

Feminism, Work, and Family

Personal and family midlife tensions and adaptations continued to form the background of my life as a newly emerging professional woman. I learned to tolerate the tensions between wanting to care for my family and wanting to follow my professional interests and opportunities. Ben's health was precarious and included a series of crises; Hyam went through a difficult divorce; Charles spent six weeks back in our home while recovering from a car accident; and Mutti lived with us during a lengthy period of slow decline. I am still grateful to Ben, my husband of forty-six years, for hanging in there with me and going through the complex realignment of our marital roles and expectations. Other marriages fell apart during similar transitions.

I found that my immersion in feminism affected not only my husband but also my adult children whom we had raised before my late awakening to feminist consciousness. While my daughter became an ally in feminist thought and in some of our woman-centered activities, my sons had reason to feel left out. My new interests, writing, and speaking exclusively on women, must have made them wonder where they fit in. I was shocked into a new awareness when I overheard my teenage grandson say: "Grandma hates men." I realized that I had some work to do to rectify that impression and began also to think about the effect of the women's movement on the men we love.

This was a time of deep personal searching and development, learning to apply a feminist analysis to my work, my personal patterns of behavior, and my self-image. It was also a time when feminist thinking was very much a work in progress.

Community Organizing

By 1976, having completed the New York State requirements for licensure and insurance reimbursements, I left the Mental Health Clinic and opened my private psychotherapy practice, first in my home, and later in a downtown building. Ruth, now a budding new attorney, and I purchased a large house at 108 W. Buffalo Street and converted it into three offices and two upstairs apartments. Ruth's legal office was upstairs. My office contained two private therapy rooms plus a group room. This room became the meeting place for the planners and doers of a number of emerging grassroots woman-centered organizations.

I was in my fifties, postmenopausal, and at the height of my creativity. I remember this decade with the excitement of taking part in a significant paradigm shift in the field of mental health and the birth of new social services for women, which are now taken for granted. I cannot resist the urge to tell this bit of Ithaca women's history and the part that I played in it.

The volunteers who later became the Ithaca Task Force for Battered Women met in my group room, following an initial meeting at the home of Nina and George Miller. Nina was then director of Suicide Prevention. A small group of clinical practitioners, psychologists, and social workers, including Mickey Goldstein, Peggy Ashford, Nina Miller, and myself, met in this office for the purpose of informing ourselves and developing services to meet the needs of battered women. It was a problem previously not talked about and not addressed by the community or mental health professionals. For some years, I co-led the regular group meetings for battered women in our group room, together with a formerly battered woman. Ruth drew up the incorporation papers for the Task Force, which is now called the Advocacy Center.

When Ruth moved on to study at Columbia University for her doctorate in Educational Administration, we rented her upstairs office to the Task Force at a much-reduced rate. It had become a large agency, grown substantially since my first anonymous contribution of

$4,000 had enabled the budding volunteer group to hire the first part-time, paid director.

I was also active in the formation of the Displaced Homemakers Agency, now called the Women's Opportunity Center. I served in succession on the boards of Ithaca's Suicide Prevention and Crisis Service, the Family and Children's Service Agency, and Planned Parenthood. My years as community representative on what was then called the Women's Studies Board at Cornell University gave me valuable insights into multidisciplinary approaches to feminist inquiry and access to the stimulating discourse of feminist thinkers in academia.

During this period, Jewish women were making waves within the Jewish establishment. When Rabbi Scott Glass took over the spiritual leadership of Temple Beth El, he appointed a committee to look into the changes necessary for fuller participation of women in religious ritual. My daughter Ruth and I served on that committee.

On the national level, starting in 1980, I attended every AWP and every FTI conference. Active on the Steering Committee of FTI, I presented at every conference, wrote for the early FTI books on Feminist

Therapy, and edited one of the book sections. I was thrilled to join the first editorial board of the new Journal of Women and Therapy. Traveling to some of the International Interdisciplinary Women's Studies Conferences where I was on the program, I had the opportunity to connect with a network of feminist thinkers and doers in Israel, Ireland, Costa Rica, and Norway. Working within the Jewish Caucuses of NWSA, the National Women's Studies Association, and AWP, I helped to introduce Jewish issues into the field of multicultural feminist discussions.

I formed significant and long-lasting friendships with distant colleagues. We saw each other rarely but were drawn together by our personal and professional involvement with issues affecting women. Among these friends, I continue to specially cherish my relationships with Ellen Cole, my coeditor and mentor, and Paula Caplan, who has become a frequent correspondent.

When I think back to my twenty-five years of professional life and writing, from 1970 to 1995, I have trouble remembering the dates and sequences of pertinent conferences and other significant markers. I also can no longer reconstruct or fill in the blanks by looking into my archives, as they are now at the Schlesinger Library at

Radcliffe in Cambridge, Massachusetts. This account is therefore less precise than I would wish. Suffice it to say that my creativity and enthusiasm were at their height during those years, from age fifty to seventy-five.

Not Retired From Life[5]

March 2009. I wake up one day to the sound of chainsaws. Instead of running away from the noise, I look out the window and stay there, mesmerized. I feel hooked by the outdoor show. I pull up a chair and stay by the window, watching, watching the workmen take down a magnificent tree. I am fascinated, totally engrossed, admiring the skill, craftsmanship, sheer body strength, agility, and acrobatic risk-taking of these tree professionals. I've been here all morning, delaying my daily walk. I cheer the workmen, I rejoice in the emerging view, and I weep for the tree, the handsome old tree, perhaps as old as I.

---

[5]   Adapted from "Retired but not Retired from Life," in *Retiring but Not Shy: Feminist Psychologists Engage their Post Careers*, eds. Ellen Cole and Mary Gergen (Chagrin Falls, OH: Taos Institute Publications, forthcoming).

Is this a metaphor for my retirement? My old age? True, I have not been cut down before my time, but I do more watching than doing, cheering and weeping as I look on from the sidelines. I am not as involved as I might have been at earlier times. I worry about the ecological impact of destroying any tree, and the energy consumed by the chainsaws. I worry about the state of the world and weep at the ever-present acts of violence against nature, against women and children, against the "other." I cheer our new president and I cheer Hillary as she starts her diplomatic journey. I watch, I cheer, I weep, I worry, and I do less, much less. I have less energy at eighty-five than I did at seventy-six when I retired, and much less than at fifty when I was at the height of my creativity. I ask myself, is this okay?

Am I, like the tree, no longer needed, taking up too much space, blocking the view, standing in the way of improvement? Unlike the tree, my own retirement was not a sudden and arbitrary cutting down, but a conscious decision to change course while still able. But there are days or moments when the sky is gray, when my joints ache, when I'm tired or ill. There are times when I feel useless, unneeded, when doubts creep in and despondency is near. But then I question the concept of uselessness; I wonder what standards to apply to the current meaning of my life.

What standards do we apply when we retire and look at our own retirement? "Productivity" and "usefulness" are buzzwords in our North American culture. Who are we when we are no longer usefully employed, when we can no longer measure our worth by what we produce or what we earn, when there's no product, no bottom line? As a therapist and as a mother, these questions are not new to me. My "product" has never been clearly defined, nor has my worth or self-esteem been measured by the product.

Before retirement, how did I as a therapist measure my product, or my success? Not by the number of "cures," not by the number of clients per day, not by the numbers in my bank account, though all of the above have at times made me feel successful, or at least useful. How did I as a mother do the same? In both roles I learned, sometimes the hard way and never completely, not to measure my own worth by my children's or my clients' success or happiness. To be completely honest, I have tried valiantly, but not always successfully, to do so. I have, in fact, felt a great deal of satisfaction when things went well for both clients and offspring, and I have indulged in self-blame when things went badly. I have, on a daily basis, derived a sense of my own worth from both roles.

How do I measure my self-worth now, in retirement from these roles, without those daily reminders of my usefulness or productivity? I have no answers to those questions, yet the absence of such answers does not trouble me. I am, on the whole, content with a profound sense of well-being that must, in itself, be part of the answer.

It takes more creativity and imagination to recognize the ways in which I still have an impact on the world around me. I have retired from my primary occupations; I have not retired from life. I have slowed down, but I have not stopped nor am I stagnant. My sphere of influence is more limited but not absent. My human interactions may even be more focused and more intense. I spend more time, both casual and intimate, with friends and family.

How do I spend my days, now that they are not structured by regular appointments? Self-care has become an important part of my daily life. I see it as my job to remain well as long as I can. I swim, I exercise, I try to keep my brain engaged. I visit doctors and physical therapists. I am protective of my aging body.

I nurture and enjoy the ever-evolving connections with my family of origin and with my children, my grandchildren, and their children. The pleasure I derive from my offspring and their growing families fills me with a deep sense of wonder and gratitude. I am wiser now than I was while raising my children. I feel that I can now reap the rewards of years in therapy and doing therapy, of consciousness raising and self-awareness. I apply a more sophisticated knowledge of social and psychological forces. In short, my current family interactions are less neurotic, less anxious, less stressful, and more enjoyable. I feel better informed and enriched by the years of having been a feminist therapist.

I have become a conveyor of family stories and genealogy, of the history of our European wanderings and displacements during the Hitler years. I also try to convey the feminist awakening in my own life journey. I write short essays, memories, and personal vignettes that embody the values that are dear to me, some of which I have collected in this book. And I continue to be involved in issues of Jewish identity, being perceived as an elder in my synagogue.

I believe that my own retirement and old age have been eased by my previous examination of aging and ageism from a feminist perspective. In these more leisurely years,

I not only look out the window, but I do a great deal of looking in and looking back. Memories of parts of my life that have been well spent help me recapture my own sense of worth. Memories of mistakes and of periods of stagnation, indecisiveness, and depression are part of the package. Knowing that those were a necessary part of growing up usually lets me return to feeling good about myself. Occasionally I lie awake with unpleasant ruminations, triggered no doubt by current life events, and I relive past tensions, traumas, events I should have handled differently. These twinges of guilt do not last or dominate my days. At times of personal loss and funerals of friends, I feel acutely lonely and think about the many loved ones who have preceded me in death. In my retirement community, death has become a normal part of living, making it easier to come to terms with my own inevitable mortality. The motto is: "Make the most of every day while you still can."

Retirement agrees with me. I like the easing of responsibilities, the freedom of being able to come and go as I please, sleeping late on a weekday if I feel like it, making spontaneous decisions. I like having more time to write, to visit, to play in the garden, watch the sunset, daydream, and be idle. I like having more time to watch and feel the beauty all around me. The quiet enjoyment of daily life has become a precious privilege.

I have had several conversations with my children and healthcare providers about my wish to be able to die peacefully without extreme interventions. Having written a detailed medical directive and arranged for a legal healthcare proxy, I feel more at ease about the process of dying and thus can live my life more fully.

Usefulness and productivity are no longer the meaningful measures of my life. What I have come to treasure in retirement and now in old age are the acts of love and caring that I exchange with those around me. A smile, a hug, a listening ear, an e-mail, a good laugh or some tears, or just plain being together and feeling connected—that is what matters now.

Ethical Will, My Legacy

Live ethically.

Love fully, openly, and mindfully.

Tell your love as often as you can, in words, smiles, gestures, deeds.

Love and care for yourself as well as you love and care for others.

Be generous to yourself, your loved ones, strangers, and even adversaries.

Find joy in honoring your heritage and family culture.

Find joy in honoring the cultures of those unlike yourself.

Express your joy and your contentment.

Keep learning in all spheres of life.

Laugh often with abandon, laugh at yourself, with others, and be whimsical.

Gripe if you have to without hurting others, then let it go.

Let go of anger, bitterness, and resentment.

Do not let others injure you or distort your sense of self.

Find beauty in the day-to-day, in ordinary sights and sounds.

Let your pores be open to the world, your eyes open to the truth, your heart open to all.

Trust your own strength, your coping, and your resilience.

Take pride without boasting and accept praise with humility.

Be not ashamed of who you are.

Affirm your accomplishments and abilities.

Be aware of your own feelings and those of others.

Be gentle with your foibles and your limitations, as well as those of others.

Be gentle with yourself and accept the times of sadness, pain, and suffering.

Mourn when you need to mourn and let yourself stop mourning.

Never forget to count your blessings.

Live life with open hands and heart.

Be not afraid of change, embrace its opportunities.

Be not afraid of living fully.

Be not afraid of death.

Addendum

Rachel Josefowitz Siegel, MSW, ACSW (Academy of Certified Social Workers)

Education

    BS, Simmons College, 1944

    MSW, Syracuse University School of Social Work, 1973

Professional Positions

    1973-76 Staff Clinical Social Worker, Tompkins County Mental Health Clinic.

    1976-95 Private Practice, Ithaca, NY.

    1984-85 Field Faculty, School of Social Work, Syracuse University.

    1995–Present Lecturer, Author

Honors

    1992   Social Worker of the Year, NASW Southern Tier Division, New York State

    1994   First Annual Award for Distinguished Contributions to the Field of Jewish Women in Psychology, awarded by the Jewish Women's Caucus of Association for Women in Psychology

1995   *Women & Therapy* vol. 16(4) dedicated to Rachel Josefowitz Siegel in honor of her seventieth birthday

1995   Included in *Feminist Foremothers in Women's Studies, Psychology, and Mental Health*, eds. Phyllis Chesler, Ellen Cole, and Esther Rothblum (New York: Haworth Press, 1995).

2005   Doris Howard Lifetime Achievement Award presented by Association for Women in Psychology

2005   Laura Holmberg Award, first recipient; Community Foundation of Tompkins County Women's Fund

Publications

Books:

Joan Hameroman Robbins and Rachel Josefowitz Siegel, eds., *Women Changing Therapy: New Assessments, Values and Strategies in Feminist Therapy* (New York: Haworth Press, 1983).

Rachel Josefowitz Siegel and Ellen Cole, *Jewish Women in Therapy: Seen but Not Heard* (New York: Haworth Press, 1991).

Rachel Josefowitz Siegel and Ellen Cole, eds., *Celebrating the Lives of Jewish Women: Patterns in a Feminist Sampler* (New York: Haworth Press, 1997).

Rachel Josefowitz Siegel, Ellen Cole, and Susan Steinberg-Oren, eds., *Jewish Mothers Tell Their Stories: Acts of Love and Courage* (New York: Haworth Press, 2000).

Articles:

"The Jew as a Woman," *Jewish Spectator* (Winter 1977).

"The Long-Term Marriage: Implications for Therapy," *Women & Therapy* 1, no. 1 (Spring 1982).

"A Midlife Journey from Housewife to Psychotherapist," *VOICES: The Art & Science of Psychotherapy* 18, no. 1 (Spring 1982).

"Women at Midlife," *Counseling and Values* 26, no. 2 (February 1982).

"Beyond Homophobia: Learning to Work with Lesbian Clients," in *A Handbook of Feminist Therapy: Psychotherapy Issues with Women,* eds. Lenore E. Walker and Lynne Bravo Rosewater (New York: Springer, 1985).

"Antisemitism and Sexism in Stereotypes of Jewish Women," in *Dynamics of Feminist Therapy.* Doris Howard, ed. (New York: Haworth Press, 1987).

"Women's 'Dependency' in a Male-Centered Value System," *Women & Therapy* 7, no.1 (1988).

"Turning the Things That Divide Us into Strengths That Unite Us," in *Diversity and Complexity in Feminist Therapy,* eds. Laura S. Brown and Maria P. P. Root (New York: Haworth Press, 1990).

Coauthor with Theo Sonderegger, "Ethical Considerations in Therapy with Older Women," in *Feminist Ethics in Psychotherapy,* eds. Hannah Lerman and Natalie Porter (New York: Springer, 1990).

"Old Women as Mother Figures," in *Woman Defined Motherhood,* eds. Ellen Cole and Jane Knowles (New York: Haworth Press, 1990).

Coauthor with Nina Katz and Amy Sheldon, "Hanukah: Lighting the Way to Women's Empowerment: A Feminist Ritual of Food, Prayer, and Ourstory-Telling," *BRIDGES, A Jewish Feminist Journal* 1, no. 2 (Fall 1990/5751): 30-31.

"Love and Work after 60: An Integration of Personal and Professional Growth within a Long-Term Marriage," and "We Are Not Your Mothers: Report on Two Groups for Women over Sixty," in *Women, Aging and Ageism,* ed. Evelyn Rosenthal (New York: Haworth Press, 1991).

"Fifty Years Later; Am I Still an Immigrant?" in *Refugee Women and their Mental Health,* eds. Ellen Cole and Esther Rothblum (New York: Haworth Press, 1992).

"Between Midlife and Old Age: Never Too Old to Learn," in *Women and Aging,* eds. Ellen Cole and Nancy D. Davis (New York: Haworth Press, 1993).

"An Immigrant Again: This Time in a Country Called Widowhood," *LILITH: The Independent Jewish Women's Magazine* 19, no. 1 (Spring 1994).

"From Immigrant to Citizen," *Simmons Review* (Winter 1995).

Coauthor with Ellyn Kaschak and Beverly A. Greene, "Three Perspectives on Racism and Anti-Semitism in Feminist Organizations: Overcoming Bias through Awareness, Mutual Encouragement, and Commitment," in *Racism in the Lives of Women: Testimony, Theory and Guides to Practice,* eds. Gloria Enguidanos and Jeanne Adleman (New York: Haworth Press, 1995).

Coauthor with Sudha Choldin and Jean H. Orost, "The Impact of Three Patriarchal Religions on Women," in *Variations on a*

Theme: Diversity and the Psychology of Women, eds. Joan C. Chrisler and Alyce H. Hemstreet (Albany: SUNY Press, 1995).

Coauthor with Theo Sonderegger, "Conflicts in Care: Later Years in the Life Span," in *Ethical Decision Making: Feminist Perspectives,* eds. Carolyn Larsen and Elizabeth Rave (New York: Guilford Publications, 1995).

"The Jewish Woman's Body: Her Sexuality, Body-Image, Self-Esteem," in *Jewish Women Speak Out: Expanding the Boundaries of Psychology,* eds. Kayla Weiner and Arinna Moon (Seattle: Canopy Press, 1995).

Coauthor with Elizabeth Traumann, "A Late Awakening," in *Feminist Foremothers in Women's Studies, Psychology, and Mental Health,* eds. Phyllis Chesler, Ellen Cole, and Esther Rothblum (New York: Haworth Press, 1995).

"Who Will Lead the Seder, Now That I Stand Alone?" in *Wisdom from the Heart: Growing Older as a Jew,* ed. Susan Berrin (Woodstock, Vermont: Jewish Lights Press, 1997).

"Silencing the Voices of Older Women," in *Ageing in a Gendered World: Issues and Identity for Women,* eds. Karen Judd, Jeannies Ash de Pou, Julia Tavares-Bucher, Tatjana Sikoska, and Juliet Solomon (Santo Domingo/New York: INSTRAW/UN Publications, 1999).

"Ageism in Psychiatric Diagnosis," in *Bias in Psychiatric Diagnosis,* eds. Paula Caplan and Lisa Cosgrove (Lanham, Maryland: Rowman & Littlefield, Inc., 2005)

"My Names," in *A Minyan of Women: Family Dynamics, Jewish Identity and Psychotherapy Practice,* eds. Beverly Greene and Dorith Brodbar (Philadelphia: Taylor & Francis, 2010).

Coauthor with Marcia Cohn Spiegel, "Older and Wiser," *BRIDGES: A Jewish Feminist Journal* 16, no. 1 (Spring 2011).

"Retired but not Retired from Life," in *Retiring but Not Shy: Feminist Psychologists Engage their Post Careers,* eds. Ellen Cole and Mary Gergen (Chagrin Falls, OH: Taos Institute Publications, forthcoming).

References

Betty Friedan, *The Feminine Mystique* (New York: W. W. Norton, 1963).

Arnold Gesell and Frances Ilg, *Infant and Child in the Culture of Today* (New York: Harper Brothers, 1943).

Roald Hoffman, *Old Wine, New Flasks: Reflections on Science and Jewish Tradition* (New York City: W. H. Freeman & Co., 1997)

Carol Gilligan, *In a Different Voice: Psychological Theory and Women's Development* (Cambridge, MA: Harvard University Press, 1993).

Jean Baker Miller, *Toward a New Psychology of Women* (Boston: Beacon Press, 1987).

CPSIA information can be obtained at www.ICGtesting.com
Printed in the USA
BVOW042108191112

305994BV00001B/14/P

9 781475 933833